The Irish public had been waiting to hear what had happened to the Dublin lads who had won the national hunt for a boy band and they got the answer when Boyzone were launched in a blaze of publicity. The group returned to appear on Ireland's *The Late, Late Show*, the scene of their shambolic, and depressing first performance. Back then, they had been six raw, local lads who were still giddy from winning the auditions when they were paraded on TV. One minute they were nobodies, the next they were expected to perform on Ireland's biggest showbiz talk show. It had been a nerve-wracking disaster, but the second visit couldn't have been more different. Boyzone were now five, well-groomed and confident young stars in the making. They were relaxed and charming and they performed their single with slick professionalism. The lads looked cool in their trendy new clothes, they danced well and the song sounded good. All those months of hard slog in the dance studio had paid off. The transformation was incredible . . .

BOYZONE

THE TRUE STORY

Rob McGibbon

B⬤XTREE

First published in 1997 by Boxtree, an imprint of Macmillan
Publishers Ltd, 25 Eccleston Place, London, SW1W 9NF and
Basingstoke

Associated companies throughout the world

ISBN 0 7522 2411 5

Cover design: Shoot That Tiger!
All photos copyright © Redferns

3 5 7 9 8 6 4 2

A CIP catalogue record for this book is available from the British
Library

Typeset by SX Composing DTP, Rayleigh, Essex
Printed by Mackays of Chatham PLC, Kent

CONTENTS

ACKNOWLEDGEMENTS

I flew to Dublin in January 1995 to interview all the lads in Boyzone at their homes. By then, they were beginning to experience the early pleasures of fame, but were concerned about burning out after gaining such instant success. All their fears were unfounded and it has been brilliant to watch them go from strength to strength since then and really crack it. Ronan, Steve, Mikey, Keith and Shane are all likeable, down-to-earth guys, who took a major gamble joining the group and have worked hard for everything they have achieved. This book charts their rise from humble beginnings in Dublin to the dizzy heights of pop fame. I hope it is a worthy reflection of their work and of the dreams they held for so many years. I also hope that there are plenty more chapters to be added in the future. Enormous praise must go to Louis Walsh, who showed unwavering belief in the boys and has worked tirelessly to get them to the top. Without him, Boyzone wouldn't have made it.

I am grateful to everyone who gave interviews and general help during my research in Dublin and, particularly to Louis, who always greeted my enquiries with charm. Special thanks to Adrian Sington and my editor Clare Hulton at Boxtree.

On a personal note, I would like to thank everyone in my family for their constant support in everything. As always, it is greatly appreciated.

INTRODUCTION

Boyzone have soared to become one of the biggest boy band sensations this decade. Following in the footsteps of New Kids On The Block and Take That, the five Irish lads have become heart-throbs all across the UK and Europe. Their rise has been incredible, even by the standards of the mad world of pop music.

It all started in the autumn of 1993 when a teenager in Dublin hit on the idea of starting Ireland's first boy band. After auditioning 300 young hopefuls, the original line up of Boyzone was found and within six months they had their first hit. By the end of 1994, their cover version of The Osmonds' 'Love Me For A Reason' had made them stars and, from there, Boyzone have continued to go from strength to strength. To date, they have chalked up two No. 1 singles, two No. 1 albums and entertained thousands with breath-taking live tours.

Life for Ronan Keating, Mikey Graham, Stephen Gately, Keith Duffy and Shane Lynch is an intoxicating rollercoaster of travelling and performing. It is a world away from their upbringing in the Northside of Dublin. But to know what they are like and what it has taken for them to get to the top, you have to go back to those roots. Only then, will you know the whole Boyzone story . . .

1

THE BLOND BOMBER
Ronan's Story

The blue electric guitar in little Ronan Keating's hands was so heavy he could barely lift it. He was small for a ten-year-old, so the guitar was as tall as him and felt like a stone slab as it sunk into his skinny thighs. His delicate fingers could hardly stretch around the neck and the rough wire strings cut into them when he tried to strum a tune. But he was determined to play that guitar. Ronan was fascinated by the weird sounds even his novice attempts could produce through the amplifier and, no matter how impossible it seemed, Ronan vowed to play it properly.

The guitar belonged to his big brother, Gary, who was four years older, and had always been keen on music. He had shown some talent for playing and had easily mastered a few chords soon after buying the instrument. Gary quickly learnt to play recognisable tunes while Ronan looked on in awe – and frustration – as his brother played the songs they had listened to on the record player. He was envious of how Gary, who was bigger and stronger, could hold the guitar expertly, just like the pop stars they watched on the television. But it made Ronan even more anxious to learn how to play. He wanted to be better than his brother and, one day, he wanted to be as good as those guys on the telly.

Despite the competitiveness the Keating brothers got on well and it was Gary's influence which sparked Ronan's passion for music. Gary had developed a fairly refined taste in music for his age and liked many classic 1960s rock and blues artists. He would play his records most evenings in his bedroom with Ronan by him listening intently. The first song Gary taught his younger brother to play on the guitar was American blues singer Ben E. King's 'Stand By Me'. It was hard at first for Ronan to learn, but, slowly, the tips of his fingers hardened and strengthened until he could comfortably press the strings to form a chord. After weeks of doggedly practising for hours each day, he was finally able to play the whole song, and sing the words, too.

Learning that guitar, and Gary's guidance in music, had a huge impact on Ronan. One album Gary played constantly was *Tea For The Tillerman* by Cat Stevens, which had been released nearly two decades earlier. It was an album few boys of Ronan's age would ever hear, but he loved it and one of the tracks became his favourite. It was a gentle, moving ballad and Ronan quickly learnt the words which he then sang all the time. Little did the ten-year-old boy realise then, however, that many years later the song he loved so much would play a critical part in his destiny. That song was called 'Father And Son'.

Ronan Keating was born on 3 March 1977, the youngest of five children. He had a happy early childhood in the Kilbarrack area of North Dublin, in Ireland. He lived less than a mile from the coast and thrived in what was a tight-knit, friendly community. He went to the nearby primary school called Bayside Juniors where he was popular and made plenty of friends. When he was eleven he moved to a local senior school. It was a period in his life which Ronan has always looked back on fondly, particularly when, in his early teens, he had a far less enjoyable time.

Gary was a big influence on Ronan's early years because all the other brothers and sisters were much older and were already leading adult lives. The four-year gap between him and Gary still meant there was a big gulf between them and, consequently, Ronan was teased a great deal and was always on the losing side when it came to fighting. Even though the fights were only silly brotherly scraps, it upset Ronan to get bruised and battered by his big brother. He would often end up in tears as he was pinned to the floor to concede submission after another 'fun' wrestling bout. There was one major advantage, however, which Ronan wouldn't appreciate for a few years: those fights with Gary toughened him up beyond his age and taught him how to look after himself. That's a skill most young boys need at some point in their lives, and few more so than Ronan.

Despite the constant brotherly bickering, there were many positive sides to Ronan's relationship with Gary and the one which had the biggest affect on his later life was Gary's love of music which influenced his younger brother. Ronan loved listening to Gary's record collection and it generated a precocious taste, where he would listen to music hardly known by most teenagers, let alone boys of Ronan's age. He loved to sing along, even though he was told by most people that he had a poor voice.

'Stand By Me', a favourite of Ronan's, was first released in 1961 but only lasted one week in the chart at No. 50. It was re-released in February 1987 and became a massive hit, going to No. 1 in the UK charts. Ronan was then approaching his tenth birthday and few lads of his age cared much what was in the charts. But Ronan was an exception and it fell to Gary to teach him how to play it on the guitar. Ronan remembers it well.

'When Gary bought his guitar I couldn't keep my hands off it,' says Ronan. 'He had an amp and I loved to make a noise. They were my earliest days in music and the first song he taught me to sing was "Stand By Me". I couldn't sing a note as a kid and I was even thrown out of the school choir because I was no good. But I used to sing every day because I loved it. I would always have my Walkman on my head and I would sing on the way to school in the mornings. I would be singing wherever I went and I didn't care if people thought I was no good. I didn't have any singing lessons – I just taught myself. But I tried not to sing too loud in the house because it drove my mum mad!'

Although Ronan enjoyed Gary's more cultured musical taste, he couldn't help but like a new group which exploded on to the music scene in January 1988 and would dominate teen pop music for two years – Bros. The good-looking blond twins Matt and Luke Goss, together with Craig Logan, became overnight sensations as their début single, 'When Will I Be Famous', went to No. 2 in the UK. The chart success more than answered the song title's question for the three lads by staying in the charts for thirteen weeks and making them seriously famous international heart-throbs.

The meteoric rise of Bros ignited teen mania among girls and left many young boys, who witnessed the band's popularity with some envy, wondering how could *they* be famous. Ronan was one lad who was deeply affected by the Bros success story. He had learnt from Gary about the hysteria surrounding great bands like The Beatles and The Rolling Stones, but he had never seen it happen to a group in his own short lifetime. For him, the Bros phenomenon happened in modern day technicolour, and it astounded him.

Soon after Ronan's eleventh birthday, Bros's next single, 'Drop The Boy', went to No. 2 and, when their third single, 'I Owe You Nothing', went to No. 1 in June, the band were established as the hottest act in the UK and Europe, as well as the Far East and Australia. The band's main following was girls, but many lads liked them, too, and Ronan became a devoted fan. He liked their cool style and enjoyed the comparison when – because of his blond hair – his pals said he looked like the twins. At least, he felt, it was good to have his own tiny piece of fame by association with the band of the moment. Ronan began to model himself on the lead singer Matt Goss and adopted his short hairstyle with a small quiff at the front. That quiff may have been the latest look, but it also earnt Ronan the nickname of Tin Tin, after the legendary adventure cartoon character, famed for the kiss curl on his forehead.

Ronan was amazed how three normal young men could have such exciting lives by doing what seemed like good fun, not work. Being a pop star seemed like the perfect job and it sparked a deep desire in Ronan that would dramatically influence his whole future. While the girl fans dreamt of dating Matt or Luke, Ronan fantasised about *being* Matt. He wanted to be famous like him; he wanted all that adulation and excitement, not to mention the extravagant lifestyle that pop stardom brought. Ronan followed the Bros career closely as they continued to hit the top-ten throughout 1988 and 1989. He also watched in amazement their slow, undignified downfall. First, they were hit by internal wrangling which ended in Craig leaving the band with a considerable pay off. It would prove to be a shrewd exit. Bros successfully continued as a duo and notched up three more hits in 1989, but the rot had begun to set in. They released only one single in 1990 and two in 1991, but all failed to make the top-ten. Finally, all the success ended in bitterness and financial failure. Luke was an emotional wreck and even the relationship between the twins was marred by the business nightmare that shattered their dreams. It emerged that they were broke, despite the string of hits. They had been ridiculously naive and exploited and they owed American Express a fortune. Even after a series of sell-out concerts, they had no money coming in. It was a sad, but all too predictable end to a bright and exciting band which had entertained so many youngsters.

Ronan was saddened to see Bros cease so harshly. It seemed crazy that two lads who had achieved so much could end up with nothing. Ronan's life had moved on considerably since the earliest hits and the height of Brosmania. But that early success had lit the touchpaper for his own pop ambitions and that was enough for him. At least, however, by following Bros he had learnt a major lesson in the pitfalls of fast fame and that alone would be valuable for him later. One burning question still remained unanswered – when would HE be famous?

While Bros were going through their own private hell, Ronan, too, was about to have his happy world turned upside down. He was thirteen and had settled in well at his secondary school when his parents dropped a bombshell: they wanted to move. His mum, Marie, and dad, Gerry, finally decided to fulfil a long-held dream to live in the country. They had grown tired of living on the fringe of a busy city. It had been fine while the kids were young, but now the three older ones were all in their twenties and had moved out to start their own lives. Gary was seventeen and he would be leaving soon, too, which just left themselves and Ronan. It seemed a perfect time to get away from the Northside of Dublin and enjoy a better quality of life in the country. It was easy for Gerry to continue his job as a salesman for a bottling company if they moved. And Marie, a hairdresser by trade, had plans to open her own salon in their new hometown. The decision was made and they chose to move to Dunshaughlin, a small town thirty miles north of Dublin, in County Meath.

It was certainly a positive move for two middle-aged parents, who yearned for a quieter life, but the move was a disaster for Ronan and couldn't have come at a worse time. He was settled at school and had all his good friends he had known for years living nearby. Now he had to start again in a new town, miles from home. On arriving in Dunshaughlin, he instantly doubted what it had to offer a teenager. The town was made up of just forty or so shops along a main road. There seemed no heart to the place, like a quaint square or side streets – just that stretch of shops, with a car repair garage, post office and a community centre. The rest of Dunshaughlin was modern, suburbia-style housing, and then it was open countryside. Ronan agreed that the houses were smart and affluent and that the atmosphere was probably safer than parts of the Northside. He also felt that it was good to be near the country, but he couldn't honestly see any attraction at all in Dunshaughlin itself for him.

If the cosmetic nature of his new hometown didn't appeal, then Ronan soon faced yet more disappointment when he struggled to settle in the area. Dunshaughlin is a closeted environment and, although the adults are friendly, the same couldn't be said for some of the children. It's hard for any thirteen-year-old to join a new school, but Ronan's worries were compounded because he was joining in a different area; not only was he the new boy, he was the outsider. He was immediately singled out by the bullies at Dunshaughlin Community College who resented his being a city boy. There was a barrage of nasty comments and one name that stuck was 'Dub', a snide abbreviation of Dubliner. To many, Ronan wasn't known by his name, but simply as 'The Dub', as if it were some inferior species.

Moving to Dunshaughlin brought huge pressure on Ronan. He hated it so much at first that it left bitter memories which lasted for years. He knew early on, however, that the only way to defend himself against the bullies was to attack. All those fights with Gary made him feel confident in his own strength and, one day, the ringleader of the main gang who picked on him pushed his luck too far. Ronan hit out and he remembers it with relish. He says, 'Nobody really liked me at that school and I was bullied all the time by a gang of boys. The leader of the bullies mucked me about too much one day and I snapped.

'I smacked him in the mouth, pushed him into a ditch and hit him a couple more times. The school was very strict about fighting and I was suspended for a week. After the week I had to write a letter apologising and asking to come back to school. The fight worked because the bully never gave me trouble again. He had a bit of respect for me and was really nice after that. But I still hated school and never did my homework. I was never any good and was a real messer – I couldn't wait to leave.'

If one move wasn't enough, shortly after arriving in Dunshaughlin, Ronan's parents decided to move again. They had found a large, red brick bungalow in an area called Dunsany, about five miles outside Dunshaughlin. That mightn't seem far, but it was even further into the country and a bigger step into isolation. The bungalow was the last in a line of properties on a narrow country road. Opposite the house, as far as you could see, were wide open fields with the odd farmhouse dotted across the landscape. It was certainly pretty and, for many, an idyllic place to live. But such isolation could hardly provide an exciting social life for young Ronan. His life became something of a boring routine. He would be driven to school by his mum in the mornings, study all day – or not, in Ronan's case – then head to her hairdressing salon in the town after school and come back with her. he would work in the salon doing odd jobs and cleaning on Saturdays to give him some pocket money.

The dramatic changes in Ronan's life did, however, gradually have some positive outcomes. Being so cut off gave him more time to practise the guitar and listen to music. It also gave him the chance to dedicate himself to athletics. Ronan had always been a fast runner, who had done well in track events and sports days at his previous schools. He had already competed at Under thirteen's level and had been crowned the National Irish Champion at 200 metres and 800 metres. Dunshaughlin College had a more advanced athletics club on its grounds than his previous school and Ronan's remarkable natural talent was quickly harnessed by its experienced coaches. Their guidance enabled him to tackle the harder, older age groups and soon Ronan was making a name for himself over several distances on the national and international running scene.

Running is in the Keating blood. Ronan's brother, Gerard, excelled at athletics too. He won countless school and county competitions and went on to become the All Ireland Champion and European

Junior Champion at 800 metres. He was so gifted and dedicated that he had won a scholarship to university in America. It was obvious that Ronan had the same inherited ability and could easily follow in his brother's running shoes.

Ronan out-ran all his contemporaries at 200, 400 and 800 metres, and was rarely off the top step of the podium. He represented Ireland against England, Scotland and Wales in the 400 metres and came second. This series of amazing track achievements brought Ronan considerable local acclaim and coverage in the newspapers. One sports writer nicknamed him The Blond Bomber in a review of a stunning performance and the name stuck. It was justified by the best times he clocked up. When he was older Ronan's best times were 200 metres in 23.4 seconds, 400 at 55 seconds and 8000 in 1 minute 52 seconds. His rivals would fear coming up against the dreaded Blond Bomber and became all too familiar with the mass of blond curls on the back of his head as he stretched away from the pack to take the winning tape.

As he matured and grew taller, his long legs, matched with his lean, wiry frame gave him the perfect weight and strength for middle-distance running. Soon, Ronan was running for Ireland on a wider junior international stage and he travelled to Belgium when he was fifteen for a major meeting where he ran in front of 30,000. He was improving all the time and his coach saw Ronan as a genuine Olympic hope for Ireland in the future. The Olympics in Sydney, Australia, in the year 2000 was the target and, as a testament to his talent, Ronan was offered a four-year scholarship at the college just outside New York where Gerard had gone. It was a fantastic opportunity where he would get the best training and enjoy some of the best facilities in the world. It was the perfect way forward for Ronan to become a major running superstar.

'Running was a huge part of my life,' he says. 'I loved nothing more than to feel the wind rushing through my hair as I won a race. I used to train all the time and was very disciplined. The people around me thought I could make it as an athlete and were totally behind me to get to the 2000 Olympics. I used to dream of winning an Olympic gold. I had passed my national goal and was aiming for an international title. The feeling I got from running in Belgium in front of all those people was incredible. I loved it so much that there was nothing I wouldn't have done for athletics. It was brilliant and the high I got from running across the finishing line first was amazing. I thought nothing could beat that feeling.'

But much to the disappointment of his coaches, Ronan soon found something which competed with the buzz of gliding over the finishing line first and which spelt the end of his Olympic dream.

His desire to sing competed against his athletics ambition. Just as his senior athletics career was getting into gear, Ronan joined an amateur pop group called Nameste. He had finally settled in at Dunshaughlin College and made several close friends, who shared his love of music. They decided to start their own band. It was only semi-serious in the beginning and served as an extension to the mundane social life teenagers had in the area. Some of the lads had instruments and they would meet for jamming sessions. It was great fun and Ronan loved it. Obviously, he liked the musical element, but, also, he enjoyed the banter and camaraderie of being in a band. It was fun, especially when contrasted to the solitary world of his homelife and the loneliness of athletics training.

The band learnt the normal run of heavy rock cover versions, as well as a few Beatles and Rolling Stones covers. At last, all those hours of practising his singing, with his Walkman on, finally paid off for Ronan as he developed into a worthy lead singer for the band. The highlight of their short career together came when they entered a talent contest at a local pub in the town and performed 'Johnny Be Goode', which Jimi Hendrix had taken to No. 5 in 1972, and another song. Ronan and his group won the £1,000 first prize. It was a staggering amount of money for a group of young lads and the victory not only made them relatively rich, but also turned them locally into mini celebrities for a while. The talent contest had a profound affect on Ronan more than anyone. It gave him a first-hand taste of the lucrative side to singing, but, above all, it showed him what it was like to be centre stage and a success in something other than in his running kit and spikes. Singing in a smoky pub certainly wasn't as healthy an environment as the track, but the buzz of the applause from the audience seemed to match the roar of the sports crowd. Ronan had loved their first short gig and he wanted more –

preferably in front of a bigger audience.

It would be hard to find two more contrasting hobbies for a teenager than singing in a teenage rock group and being a national athletics star. Being fit helped Ronan give energetic performances on stage as his band followed their talent contest success with a few gigs. But late nights in dingy clubs, eating junk food, did nothing for his track performance and, perhaps inevitably, his ability and his attitude slackened as he enjoyed the fun of being in the band and having a more exciting social life. That social life took a further turn for the better when his parents decided to move once more, this time nearer to Dublin. They had decided their jaunt to the country hadn't been the blissful dream they had hoped for, realising they missed city life. Even though Ronan had started to enjoy himself in Dunshaughlin, he couldn't wait to get back amongst his old friends and return to his old school.

The return to the Northside spelt the end of his band, but it gave Ronan the chance to dedicate himself to athletics again. He continued to win many races and secured his place at university in America. But, although he was being groomed to win Olympic glory for his country, Ronan couldn't help but wrestle with the thrill of standing at the top of the podium and that of being on stage with a microphone in his hand and the audience at his feet.

Little did he know that fate had already decided the track for his life to follow. Ultimately, he would make Ireland incredibly proud of his achievements, but the coveted gold he would eventually win wouldn't be in the shape of a small sporting medal.

2

THE VON TRAPP FAMILY
Mikey's Story

There was always a party going on in the small semi-detached house where the Graham family lived and the neighbours were well used to music and singing blaring out of its windows at all hours. Everyone knew how much the Grahams loved a party, so the noise was never a problem. If there was a celebration locally for a birthday, or an engagement, a crowd of die-hard revellers would invariably end up continuing into the early hours at the Graham house. It was open-house there, and the family liked nothing more than a group of cheerful people singing and dancing in the front room.

It was this love of singing and their carefree attitude which earnt the Grahams their nickname, the Von Trapp Family, after the song-loving family in the classic 1965 film *The Sound of Music*. In the movie, the Austrian Von Trapp children were taught to sing under the tuneful guidance of Julie Andrews, who then helped them flee their war-torn country across the mountains into Switzerland. In the best traditions of Irish Catholics, the Grahams were a large family, too, with five girls and two boys, with only eight years separating the eldest, Yvonne, and the baby of the family, Michael. Like the Von Trapps, they were also happy and close.

Although Mikey and his family were far from living in the trauma of the Second World War, they were certainly not living in the best circumstances. Their house was in a none too prosperous area called Coolock, on Dublin's Northside, with sprawling estate blocks across the road. Their dad, Billy, a carpenter by trade, was the head of

11

maintenance at one of Dublin's department stores and he did as many hours as possible to bump up his pay packet in order to keep such a large family. Feeding and clothing seven children on a modest wage wasn't easy, so there were few luxuries and they led far from extravagant lives. Their mother, Sheila, did cleaning work when she could, but couldn't take a full-time job to bring in extra money, because there was too much to do keeping the family in order. But the lack of money was no problem for the Grahams. They didn't have fancy lifestyles with expensive foreign holidays, but their house was always happy and full of fun, even if it was very cramped. The five girls shared their main bedroom at the front of the house, all in bunk beds, while Mikey shared the small room next door with his brother Niall, who was eight years older. Mum and dad had the back bedroom. It was hardly an ideal set-up, but what the house lacked in space, it made up for in atmosphere. It was a bustling household, full of banter and humour, and the mornings, in particular, were a manic whirl as the kids tried to get ready for school. They battled through a tight rota to use the bathroom and the house was filled with the incessant whining of a hairdryer from the girls' bedroom.

Evenings were great fun, too. The family would sit round chatting for ages after their dinner and the house became even more cramped with the selection of friends who gathered there, too. Everyone loved going to the Graham house and the family were always so upbeat they didn't need the excuse of a formal party for there to be singing. Sheila loved singing and, with five happy, extrovert girls – including the twins, Clare and Debbie – a song was never far away. Even at night, when it was well past bedtime for the younger children, the singing would start. It was an atmosphere Mikey remembers fondly.

'My house was always full of music and fun,' he says. 'We would all be lying in bed late at night and the bedroom doors would be open. There was always plenty of chat and noise from the girls' room. One of them would start singing, then a few of the others would join in, then Niall and I would start up. Finally, my parents would start singing in the back bedroom. It would be around midnight and the whole house would be singing. It was mad, but really great fun. We loved a good sing-song which is why we were called the Von Trapps.'

Mikey was born on 15 August 1972 but it wasn't a smooth, worry-free arrival. He was seriously ill soon after being allowed home and had to go back into hospital for specialist care. There were fears that he might die, but, thankfully, he pulled through and was finally given a clean bill of health and allowed home for good. He was bound to be pampered as the baby in such a house full of girls, but the trauma of his early months guaranteed his extra attention. It was a warm and secure environment to be brought up in and Mikey had a happy, busy early childhood.

Like Ronan, Mikey's early interest in music was influenced by his elder brother. Niall and Mikey shared a room and, despite such a big age gap, they became close. Because music was such a feature in the Graham household, their mum bought them both harmonicas when they were kids, which they learnt to play very quickly. But Mickey's passion for pop music took hold when he was just seven years old as a new British group arrived on the world music scene in 1979 with all sirens blaring – The Police.

The band's first hit was 'Roxanne', which went to No. 12 and was following by a No. 2 with 'Can't Stand Losing You'. Their first No. 1 followed soon after with 'Message In A Bottle', which established them as the hottest act in pop of the moment. Niall liked them first and bought all the singles and the first album, *Outlandos D'Amour*, and played them continuously in the bedroom. Like Ronan, Mikey followed his big brother's lead in music. He couldn't afford his own records, so he listened to Niall's. There is little chance that a seven-year-old would independently find his own way into music, but Niall's interest opened Mikey's young ears. They learnt the words together and became devoted Police fans. One of Mike's favourites was 'Walking On The Moon', the band's second No. 1. But it was the charismatic blond lead singer, Sting, who mesmerised Mikey. Each time The Police were on *Top Of The Pops* singing their latest hit, Mikey would stare closely at Sting's cool performance. The Police were as influential on Mikey's future as Bros would be on Ronan years later. Mike was so captivated by the band's success and Sting's talent that it ignited his desire to be a pop star. Even today he acknowledges Sting as one of his all-time great heroes. Niall remembers, 'Mikey was knocked out by Sting. He thought he was so cool and I remember him saying something like "I want to be a star like Sting" after he had watched The Police on the television one night. He was only a little kid but it had a big affect on him.'

Sheila Graham was eager to encourage both her sons' interest in music, so, despite money being tight, she bought them an acoustic guitar to share. It was a Spanish-style instrument and they loved it. Niall enjoyed playing, but, just like the Keating brothers, the younger lad showed a more instinctive desire to learn. Mikey practised for hours, slowly mastering the chords until he could play complete songs. One of the first songs he learnt to play was The Beatles' 'Yesterday', and 'Mull of Kintyre', Paul McCartney's massive hit of 1977 with Wings. He also tried his favourite Police songs, but they were more difficult to mimick because of the electric guitar. Niall looks back on Mikey's early 'career' in music: 'I remember that guitar our mum bought us. It was only a cheap one, but it was brilliant and Mikey spent ages teaching himself to play – he was really dedicated. There was something inside him that drove him on to learn.'

It seemed from the moment Mikey discovered The Police and could play the guitar, he was determined to be a singer like his hero Sting. He played the records constantly and he loved the band's second album, *Regatta De Blanc*. When Mikey was eight, he bought his first record out of his pocket money – it was The Police's single, 'De Do Do Do, De Da Da Da', which went to No. 5 in December 1980.

For such a young lad, Mikey showed a precocious inner belief that one day he would indeed make it. Years later, when his childhood dreams were a reality thanks to Boyzone, Mikey said, 'I always believed that my life was leading to something like this. I don't why or how, but I always thought I would make it in music.' Niall can bear testament to that early vision and vividly remembers Mikey predicting his destiny when he was a boy. The moment came when Mikey was listening to Niall and his friends chat about their futures. They were all around eighteen years old and were wondering which jobs they would do when they left school. It is a conversation that still sticks in Niall's mind today.

'My friends and I were sitting in our house talking about what apprenticeships we would go into once we had finished school. Most of us were thinking of learning a trade, like engineering, carpentry or car mechanics. We were all aiming for the normal sort of jobs lads think about. Mikey was always hanging out with me and my friends, even though he was so much younger, and he was listening to our conversation. We asked him what he wanted to do when he was grown up and he said, "I'm going to be a pop star."

'We all laughed at him. He was only about ten at the time and it was the sort of thing a young kid would come out with. It was like him saying he wanted to be an astronaut or a pilot. We said, "Oh yeah, in your dreams, Mikey." We couldn't take him seriously, so we all took the mickey out of him. But he was totally serious and really stuck up for himself. He said, "You wait and see, I'll show you, I'll show you. I'm going to be famous and have my own mansion . . ." It was like he really believed he would be a star some day, even way back then. We joked with him and told him to stop dreaming, but he wouldn't have it and got annoyed. In the end we said, "Okay, we hope it comes true for you." But, of course, none of us thought it would,' says Niall.

'There was always something about Mikey. He really believed he was going to be famous one day. He had a vision in his head and it all started with The Police. When he saw them he realised there was a world out there that was exciting and out of the ordinary – and he wanted it. He even started practising his autograph when he was a kid, just so that he knew what to do when he was famous. I suppose all youngsters do that at some stage, but he really meant it.'

Mikey was many years away from becoming a pop hero, or even starring in his own amateur band, but, luckily for him, his eager thirst for performing was quenched thanks to his sister Catherine. Among the family of extroverts in the Graham household, Catherine was one of the bigger personalities. She had been the first to show genuine singing ability when she was young so she joined the Gaiety Theatre in the town centre. She appeared in several big musicals, including the lead role in *Annie*, the heart-warming tale of the little red-haired orphan.

Mikey loved watching his sister on stage and saw the tremendous buzz she got from acting. He knew he wanted to be on stage, too, so he joined the Billie Barry School of Theatre and Dance, which had a long-standing reputation in Dublin for nurturing young talent with drama lessons after school hours. Mikey enrolled with his best friend Shane Wood, and they were instantly earmarked as the devils of their class. Mikey says, 'I was a handful for my mum to look after when I was a boy, so I went to drama school to get me out of the way, not that I was a little villain or anything. I really got into it and the teachers liked Shane and me because we were good characters and such little rascals. The other lads in the school were real idiots, who sucked up to the teachers and were a bit feminine. Me and Shane were real little lads and we didn't give a damn about behaving nicely. I think they liked us because we were different. We got on very well and did a lot of shows.'

Mikey stayed at the Billie Barry school for several years and appeared in pantomimes, which toured around the Dublin area, as well as countless other plays and musicals. Belonging to the school led to other, even more exciting avenues for Mickey and his friend – television fame. They were hired to appear on childrens' telly shows, Ireland's famous *The Late, Late Show*, and were even given small parts in television adverts. By the time Mikey was nearing his fifteenth birthday, he had already built up a considerable background as a young performer and the people in his local area followed his growing career.

'They all thought I was a celebrity when I was younger,' he says. 'Everyone watched us when we were on television and came to see our stage shows. It was great fun and our parents were really proud.'

Mikey lapped up all the intoxicating applause from the audiences at the shows and was intrigued by the complexities of television. It was an incredible deluge of experiences of life in the entertainment world for such a young lad and it was perfect ground work for what lay ahead.

Despite the busy involvement with the drama school, not to mention the normal weight of school work, Mikey still had time to develop one of his other main interests – kick boxing. He trained regularly at a kick boxing club and managed to achieve a standard high enough to compete in local competition. The lads at the club would train on the beaches outside Dublin, especially when it was cold in winter because it helped develop discipline and physical toughness. Mikey learnt to take care of himself and had quick hands and feet, but, one day, he breached the rules of restraint during a sparring session with a contemporary.

'I was very sporty as a kid and really enjoyed kick boxing. We were on the beach having a light sparring session when one of the lads hit me. I wasn't very happy about it and I lashed out. I hit him hard in the face and a tooth came through his lip. I was really made and I had to be dragged off him by the others. I was in trouble because the sport is as much to do with discipline as fighting,' Mikey says.

'I was quite good at kick boxing but I wouldn't class myself as Bruce Lee or anything. I have had fights in the streets once or twice but nothing too serious and I haven't put anyone in hospital. I used to go into competitions and the best I did was when I won three fights in a knockout competition, but lost the fourth. I still did well to get through all those rounds.'

Mikey finally left the Billie Barry school and devoted more time to his first love, music. Deep down, he still felt his destiny lay in music, but he also knew that belief alone doesn't make someone famous. It takes talent, hard work and years of dedication, too. Thanks to his time at drama school, he had proved he had the ability to perform in front of an audience; he knew he had the dedication to pursue fame – the priority now was to develop his musical ability.

Although he was far from mastering the guitar, Mikey wanted to progress musically, so his parents bought him a basic electronic keyboard one Christmas. He was determined to conquer that instrument and would lock himself away in his bedroom to teach himself to play. Even on weekend mornings, when his pals were out in the streets playing football and generally hanging out, Mikey would be alone in his room learning a new song. Some days he would take the keyboard and its amplifier out into the shed at the end of the small back garden, which was linked up to the electricity in the house. The seclusion helped him concentrate. His sister Catherine had joined her own rock band called Hit and Run, and Mikey began writing songs for them. And when he was old enough he formed his own group. He was the lead singer and principal songwriter, although the group preferred to play cover versions.

Being in the band gave Mikey the chance to be the main star, as opposed to one in a cast of many as he had been in stage productions and his telly appearances. It was good fun and the lads managed to earn some money from gigs in pubs and local community halls, but it was such a pittance that the cash normally disappeared on travelling expenses and beer before the night was over. Unfortunately, an amateur rock group was no way to earn a living so, as Mikey reached his seventeenth birthday, he had to consider his future seriously.

Years before he had confidently predicted to Niall and his pals that when he left school he was going to be a pop star. He told them he wasn't going to bother with apprenticeships and normal jobs, he was going to be rich and famous, just like Sting. But Mikey couldn't escape the stark reality that it hadn't happened. Well, not yet, anyway. Sure, he had achieved a lot in the world of entertainment for a teenager, and had enjoyed some fame locally, but he was a long way from the dream of making his living from music. To make it more worrying, his years of busy pursuits outside school meant his studies had been neglected so much that he was leaving with few academic qualifications. Mikey's options were alarmingly limited and he had to accept that he would have to get a normal job. It was a route Niall and his mates had faced years earlier, while young Mikey had talked confidently of pop stardom. The reality seven years on was that the dreaming had to stop, at least for now.

Mikey had always shown a genuine interest in cars. His first car was a clapped-out orange Fiat, which he spent ages tinkering with. He learnt a lot from trial and error on his own car and becoming a mechanic seemed about the only everyday job he really fancied doing. It seemed a fairly laid back and fun job and eventually he was taken on by a firm called Annesley Motors.

Mikey worked with a good bunch of lads and enjoyed the banter of the work place. He would entertain them by singing along to songs which blared out of the radio in the garage all day long and they joked that he should be a singer. The lads may have laughed about him becoming a star, but inwardly Mikey was still deadly serious. He knew that being a mechanic was only a temporary measure and that one day the oil and engine grease etched into his skin would be gone, and the voice coming from the radio would be his.

3

THE SHY STAR

Steve's Story

One common contradiction exists in many of the world's greatest entertainers: they are hugely confident, larger than life characters in front of an audience, but, once the spotlight fades, they are introverted people who retreat into a shell of shyness. This anomaly is true of Stephen Gately.

As a little boy, Steve was timid and quiet and would often have a worried look in his big blue eyes. He was a small lad who appeared to shirk attention, but, lurking just under the surface there was a big extrovert waiting for the opportunity to grab the limelight. He was the type who would be painfully silent if, for example, anyone new such as a friend of his parents came into his house. But, once he had worked out the situation and felt sure that the stranger posed no threat, Steve would emerge as the fun showman who would happily tell jokes and sing for their amusement. One trick he favoured was to sing using one of his mum's slippers as a microphone.

Steve was born on 17 March 1976. He was the second youngest in the family and has three brothers and one sister. Like Mikey, he wasn't from a wealthy home and was brought up in Seville Place, one of the rougher areas of Dublin's Northside. Seville Place is only a few miles from the bustling, smart centre of Dublin, but it bears little resemblance to the wealthy streets of the Southside. It is known for its sprawling, run-down housing estates, and Steve's first home was a tiny flat on such an estate. Social problems are commonplace in any neglected section of an inner city and Seville Place has become notorious for a high crime rate and an escalating drug problem among its youth. Disillusioned, unemployed teenagers, with few prospects for a bright future, roam the streets day and night, creating what can be an oppressive atmosphere. It's a tough environment for any child to grow up in and many are caught in its negative downward spiral. But, for Steve Gately, the opposite was true. The problems he saw in sharp focus throughout his early years, and the odds that seemed so heavily stacked against him, inspired him to seek a different life. He became determined to break away from the gloom and not become just another sad, vacant face with no ambition on the street corner. He wanted to make a name for himself.

Steve was always sensitive and his mother, Margaret, wasn't surprised when, like a typical mummy's boy, he cried his eyes out when he had to leave her for his first day at infant school. He took longer than the other children to gain his confidence and was one of the quietest in the class, and fearful of speaking out loud. One of his strengths, however, was reading. Maybe it was the lack of space and shabby surroundings of his home that drew Steve to the fantasy world of literature. It provided him with an exciting escape and his particular love was for adventure books by Enid Blyton, the doyenne of children's stories. He read through her collection voraciously and even read some of his favourites, such as *The Enchanted Garden*, more than fifty times. If Steve was ever feeling down, or frustrated by the claustrophobic environment, he would bury his face in a book and be transported to another, more thrilling world where there were deep forests, fun and danger. Steve was a dreamer and reading unleashed his imagination. He says, 'I love Enid Blyton books and the adventures her characters had. They were so exciting and I would lose myself in them. *The Enchanted Garden* was my favourite.'

When he wasn't dreaming of some far off fantasy world, Steve was occupied with the big worry in his life: how was he going to escape the drudgery of life in Seville Place for real, and for good. He had no idea how he could make that happen, but then he discovered an exciting new hobby which showed him a novel way of earning a living – acting.

Steve's powerful imagination was noticed by a drama teacher

called Mrs Higgins. She could see Steve's natural flair for improvisation and creativity, as well as his fascination for make believe. She instinctively knew that the shy boy had a big personality waiting for its chance to bloom. Mrs Higgins wanted to develop his raw talent for performing, and coaxed him into becoming more involved in junior school drama classes. It was the spark of encouragement he needed so badly and Steve grasped it enthusiastically. He quickly grew in confidence and, even though he was still timid in academic lessons, during drama he was articulate and full of himself. Soon he was taking on the leading roles in school plays, and his naturally high singing voice began to shine through. Steve says, 'Mrs Higgins really changed me – she gave me so much confidence in myself. I am very grateful for all the help and guidance she gave me.'

Steve was a willing pupil who thrived on the excitement of preparing for a show and actually enjoyed the horrendous nerves which built up before going on stage. He lapped up the attention, none more so than in his biggest role in a junior school production – as the lead in *Joseph And His Amazing Technicolour Dreamcoat*. The witty biblical musical, written by the British composers Andrew Lloyd Webber and Tim Rice, has provided the perfect role for many young performers who have since become successful entertainers. Gary Barlow, the lead signer and driving force behind Take That, starred as Joseph when he was eleven and the heady experience fuelled his ambition to be famous. The same was true of Steve. He revelled in the colourful costumes, the make-up and, above all, he loved the long applause he earned from his performance in the lead role. The adrenalin from singing his solo spots under the spotlight in front of a large audience was intoxicating. It was like nothing he had ever experienced and he was left needing that high again. The teachers who had only ever seen the quiet side of Steve marvelled at his transformation from the shy boy to the confident young star of the stage.

When he was older, Steve joined the Gaiety Theatre group in the city centre, where Mikey also performed, but they were in different age groups and neither remember meeting there. Steve enjoyed performing at the Gaiety and, although he wasn't a star in those shows, the experience in front of bigger, more discerning audiences was invaluable. Steve's love of acting and singing also featured in his social life outside school and the Gaiety. He was eager to pass on his love of performing and would spend many evenings teaching drama to youngsters at the local youth centre. Seville Place was starved of the sort of facilities and guidance that would encourage bored kids to be interested in the arts, so it was a challenge for Steve to embark on such a tough task. He directed short plays and began choreographing dance routines when he started his own disco dance troupe called Black Magic. Again, he shone out as the most talented of the group, thanks to his natural rhythm and fast feet. He had the skill to dance complicated sequences at top speed, yet still look cool. Black Magic became a serious pastime, with Steve entering the group into competitions all over Dublin. It proved a worthwhile grounding for his future with Boyzone and Steve loved the sweet taste of success with Black Magic when they won the all-Ireland disco dance finals.

To add to Steve's busy schedule, he branched out in the modelling business when he was fifteen and signed up with an agency. He was a good looking teenager and photogenic, so he easily got work modelling fashion for some of the big shops in Dublin.

While Steve was having great fun with his growing modelling career, as well as performing at the youth centre and in the Gaiety productions, his very active life outside school had a bad effect on his studying. Predictably, his interest in academic subjects was minimal as his heart focused on a future on the stage or in music. He couldn't see how chemistry or maths lessons, for example, could possibly help him become a performer. His problems at his secondary school were made worse by strict teachers who believed physical punishment, such as caning, could cure a pupil's poor attitude. This archaic form of discipline put Steve off school even more and made him long to leave.

'Some of the teachers at my school used to have canes just in case anyone got out of line. I used to dread going to school, especially when I didn't have my homework done or we had tough exams. My most enjoyable day at school was the day I left,' says Steve.

A low-budget film gave Steve another small taste of fame when he

Ronan struts his stuff
in Boyzone's first
major tour in 1995.

Shane makes sure the
show goes on despite
a broken ankle.

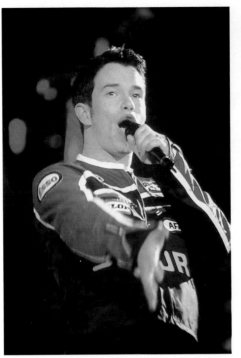

Steve, the shy dreamer who always wanted to be a star, comes alive under the spotlight.

Keith takes a breather during a frantic live show.

Mikey hits centre stage at the Labatts Apollo in London.

The boys perform at a radio roadshow.

Ronan sings 'Love Me For A Reason' at the Smash Hits Awards in 1994.

Steve smiles during a promotional performance at the Virgin Megastore.

The five lads have become as close as brothers since joining the group.

Shane and
Mikey sport
early hairstyles.

Ronan beckons
the girls with
his sweet tunes.

Mikey and Shane bid farewell after another red hot gig.

In casual clothes, Keith takes
pop fame in his stride.

Shane bleached his
quiff and shaved
one eyebrow for
a star image.

The lads cement their place in pop fame for The Wall of Hands at London's Rock Circus.

The boys arrive in colourful style at the MTV Awards in 1996.

was sixteen. It was called *The Commitments* and went on to become a worldwide box office hit. Its story followed the ups and downs of a hard-up Irish soul group trying to break into the big time. It was a humorous film, which showed the band dreaming of fame and fortune as they squabbled and struggled to make it, only, in the end, to fail. It was set in the Northside of Dublin, so, naturally, the director, Alan Parker, headed to the area to make the movie. Because of his limited funds, Parker was restricted to a limited cast and cheap location shoots. One luxury in particular that he couldn't afford was hiring hundreds of extra for certain scenes. He was faced with a major dilemma for the opening sequence, which featured one of the principle characters walking through a packed street market. It required several hundred extras to fill the set and was impossible for Parker to finance. The solution he found was to invite locals to become 'stars' for the day. It was a great idea, which generated a huge response and gave Parker a ready-made – and free – street crowd. The only extra cost was a few thousand pounds for the catering, which was a small price to pay.

Steve, his mum, and their friends were among those who joined the crowd scene in the hope of clocking up a few seconds in that magical fifteen minutes of fame that the artist Andy Warhol said everyone will have in their lifetime. When the film-makers arrived, it was like the circus had come to town and Steve was awestruck by the glamour of the actors and the enormity of film-making, watching as the big trucks rolled in and the crews rigged up the cameras and lighting. For most of the crowd it was just a fun day out, but the experience had a major impact on Steve. Only a few would manage to get their faces actually on the screen and most would end up on the cutting-room floor, or as blurred images in the background. But Steve and his mum were luckier than most. They managed to get near the camera shot for one of the scenes and, apparently, they appear in the final edit, but it's impossible to tell – even by watching a video of that scene in the film in slow motion.

As the memories and excitement of that day on the set of *The Commitments* faded, Steve was inwardly determined that it wouldn't be his only moment of fame. He was determined to get his full fifteen minutes . . . and a lot more. The story of *The Commitments* was fittingly ironic because Steve would also follow the path of the dreamers in the imaginary band. He and the four other Northside lads who would become Boyzone would struggle at first, but, unlike the film, their bid for stardom would have a far happier ending.

4

THE SPORTSMAN
Keith's Story

Keith Duffy's home of Donaghmede is a little more than four miles from Seville Place, but the contrast in the two places is far greater than the short geographical distance. Seville Place and its grey buildings is a world away from the affluent suburb of Donaghmede where most of the homes are large detached houses in tidy, tree-lined streets. Expensive new cars fill many of the driveways and the neighbourhood has a safe, respectable atmosphere with none of the negative problems of the inner city. Steve had to cope with the problems of his town, but Keith enjoyed the security of a predominantly middle-class area. The Duffys, however, weren't rich and their comfortable house was only maintained by both parents working hard. Keith's mum, Patricia, was a hairdresser who ran her own salon, and his dad, Sean, was the manager of Frawley's, one of Dublin's largest department stores. They needed both salaries to keep Keith and his two brothers – one older and one younger – in a good lifestyle.

Keith was blessed with a secure family environment and it helped him develop one of his most prominent characteristics – confidence. He was always a super-confident child and, once he had got over the initial worry of going to school, he thrived there and became a good pupil. At times, he could be too boisterous and the teachers would often have to keep him in check, but no matter how stern the reprimand, Keith would soon bounce back to his fast-talking cheeky ways. Keith had unshakeable self belief and it helped him do well in all aspects of school life. He was an all-rounder who was academically bright and excelled at all sports. In short, Keith was one of those young boys who was good at everything and, to top that, he was blessed with handsome looks which made him popular with the girls. If Keith had one downfall, it was that he knew he was talented and so presented an almost arrogant front. This cocky attitude didn't endear him to everyone and some rival boys, in particular, took a dislike to him. They envied his talent and popularity and took revenge by bullying him. Like Ronan, Keith wasn't prepared to take any rough treatment and was frequently involved in fights while defending himself. He wasn't big for his age, but he was fast and fearless, so he rarely ended up on the losing side.

'I was one of the better-looking lads at school and it made some of the others jealous. I had no problem getting girls at the discos, which upset some guys. They were being stupid and I was happy to fight to stick up for myself,' Keith says.

Sport was the focal point of Keith's early teenage years. He developed a tight group of friends who were all good at games and, because he was always in a gang of strong, athletic lads, the bullying problem soon disappeared. He took up the two main national sports in Ireland, hurling and Gaelic football, and his raw ability quickly shone through. He had good coordination and lightening quick pace, which made him a strong forward player in hurling and a dangerous attacking midfielder in football. Keith's school team dominated the inter-school matches at both sports and won their area championships. He also represented Dublin City's hurling side for three years at various age levels up until the under eighteens, and collected a horde of medals and trophies after success in major fixtures. Keith lived for his sport and hoped to be a professional hurling player. He may well have been good enough to make it, especially as his physique developed in his late teens, but his playing career was brought to an abrupt and worrying halt when he was seventeen after he suffered a bad injury. Hurling is played at a furious pace, with each player using a wooden stick to hit the hard ball. Most players wear head protection, but Keith had chosen not to wear his this fateful day and, sure enough, he was hit on the head. He still remembers the accident vividly and recalls how it nearly led to serious complications.

'I got a crack on the skull during the game and it gave me a nasty headache, which still hurt much later when I was at home. I thought it would wear off, so I didn't do anything about it, but a couple of days later, I still had a headache and it was getting worse. I couldn't get rid of it and I started to worry what was happening to me. I didn't associate it with the accident on the field because it didn't seem that bad at the time – there had been no bleeding or anything – but now I couldn't even stand up without getting a bad migraine. I thought I might have a brain tumour or something, so I went to the hospital for some scans. It turned out that I had a hairline crack on my skull. The doctors told me that if I hadn't gone in it could have got pretty serious. I was kept in hospital for two weeks for treatment. I was lucky it hadn't got worse, but I was really fed up because it meant I couldn't play any more. I loved the game and had loads of trophies. I hated having to stop.'

If the crack to his head wasn't bad enough, Keith was dealt another health blow as while he was in hospital the doctors also discovered he had a murmur on his heart. The condition means his heart misses a beat every now and then. It's not an uncommon problem and isn't life threatening, but the doctors made him aware that he wasn't to put himself under too much physical strain. Reluctantly, Keith gave up competitive sport, but it provided him with time to do a regular Saturday job and pursue his other interest – music.

As a child, Keith had always been involved in acting and singing. He loved the drums and, when he was a little boy, he joined a marching band, typically taking centre stage at the front. Like Steve and Mikey, he enrolled in a respected drama school in Dublin where he appeared in big musical productions and pantomimes. Again, it was his precocious confidence which made him enjoy the pressure and excitement of being on stage. His involvement with the drama school boosted his confidence even further, so, when his primary school put on shows, Keith made sure he was never far from the main spotlight.

Keith was a good drummer and he saved up enough money from part-time work to buy his own drum kit. He joined an amateur pop group, Toledo Moon, with some close pals and they performed the normal run of cover versions of rock classics in rundown community halls. Although he loved being in the band, he hated being so far from the limelight behind the drums. He yearned to be out the front.

'I loved the idea of being on stage and I used to put on a leather jacket at home and stand in front of the mirror and pretend I was Freddie Mercury from Queen. It was great fun playing the drums in the band, but anyone would rather be the star of the show,' says Keith.

Although he came from a relatively well off family, he had to work for his pocket money throughout his teenage years. His dad wasn't prepared to give him handouts so Keith always did various jobs for a few pounds to keep him going. He finally settled on a regular Saturday job at the department store where his dad was manager. The money gave him more freedom socially and he began to get into the vibrant nightclub scene in Dublin. He loved dancing and would often be found on the stage or high on a podium so he got the maximum attention from other clubbers. It was this blatant exhibitionism which would unexpectedly provide his chance to join Boyzone.

Keith lapped up the physical exertion from dancing and it helped stem the frustrating void he had felt from giving up sport. But, to keep himself in even better physical shape, he joined a local gym and began regular weight-training sessions. He trained for two hours, five nights a week and soon built up a well-defined muscular physique. Those bulging muscles led to a very odd job offer and the sessions at the gym helped Keith strike up a friendship with someone who would have a major effect on his life. That person was Shane Lynch and the job the weight training landed Keith was as a stripper!

Keith had known Shane for years. They lived in the same area and, by coincidence, Keith had gone out with one of Shane's sisters, Alison, for a short time. The two lads were never close friends because Shane was two years younger, but they knew each other well enough to have a brief chat if they saw one another about town. When Shane bumped into Keith in the gym one evening, he knew he had found the perfect candidate for a job he and a good friend had been offered. They had been asked to perform a striptease show in the function room above a pub for a group of women on a hen night, but they needed one extra man. Keith was ideal. He looked good and easily had the guts to go through with such a nerve-wracking job. Keith immediately accepted when Shane told him he would earn £50 for just fifteen minutes work. He was used to working for anything up to ten hours in the department store for half, so he was pleased to say yes, even if it meant stripping to a G-string in front of screaming women. If anything, the bizarre nature of the work was as much an incentive as the money. He knew he was good looking and felt it would be the easiest money he had ever earnt.

For the show, Keith had to dress up as Father Christmas, while Shane hired a priest's costume. All they had on beneath their costumes were starched collars and bow ties and G-strings. Keith did his raunchy strip to the Right Said Fred hit song 'I'm Too Sexy', and he still laughs when he remembers the night.

'It was amazing and very funny. We whipped a few of the girls and had some laughs. I was in very good shape then and enjoyed myself. The money was incredible because I had never earnt so much before in such a short time. I was up for doing more shows, but I don't think Shane enjoyed it that much. He was very embarrassed. The girls loved it and some of them had seen The Chippendales before but said we were better. We could have made a fortune if we had done some more,' he boasts.

Sadly, Keith and Shane's stripping career came to an exhilarating but premature end. Keith had to concentrate on a more serious future and things looked promising after he collected five honours passes in his Leaving Certificate, the exam grading system in Irish schools. He easily qualified for an architecture course at college and quickly showed a natural flair for design, which resulted in him passing the first year's exams with good grades.

It seemed that Keith was set for a lucrative and steady career as an architect, but those ambitions crumbled once he heard that his old stripping pal Shane Lynch was starting a pop group.

5

THE WHIZZ KID

Shane's Story

Out of all the lads who eventually became Boyzone, Shane Lynch was probably the least likely candidate for a pop group. All the others had at some point in their lives craved the spotlight, either in acting or music, or both. Ronan, Mikey and Keith had joined various amateur groups and Steve had loved acting and then achieved a certain degree of success in a dance troupe. In contrast, Shane had never been drawn to the world of entertainment. If anything, he actively avoided such things as school plays, drama groups and teenage bands, so it seems ironic that he should eventually be one of the catalysts to the creation of Boyzone.

Shane had the normal interests most boys have while growing up, like riding bikes, playing sport and generally messing around with a bunch of pals in his area. He was born on 3 July 1976, the only boy among five sisters, which may have accounted for his desire to spend so much time with his friends out on the streets of Donaghmede. He was a mischievous tearaway but never so bad that he got into serious trouble. In a house full of women, Shane only had his dad, Brendan, as a male influence and role model, so it was inevitable Brendan became something of a hero to him throughout his childhood. His dad owned a successful car repair garage business which provided the family with a large home and a good lifestyle, with annual family holidays abroad. The success of the garage also enabled Brendan to pursue his main hobby – car racing.

Brendan's passion was for stock car racing, one of the wildest forms of motor sport where part of the rules, and the fun, is to crash into other vehicles in pursuit of the lead. It's a nerve-jangling sport and not for the faint-hearted, but Brendan loved it and his enthusiasm rubbed off on his son. At weekends, Shane would travel with his dad to race meetings all over Ireland and watch in amazement at the lawless, anything-goes mania that is peculiar to stock-car racing. He would marvel at the speed at which his dad and the other competitors would hurtle around the tight tracks and gasp as they smashed into each other, only to continue on with the race as if nothing had happened. Shane saw some spectacular crashes which resulted in cars being withdrawn from races, and would look on in admiration as the drivers climbed out of their crumpled wrecks unscathed and unperturbed by the shock of the accident. If anything, they emerged as heroes and were greeted with loud roars from the crowds.

Shane was affected by what he saw. He became hooked on the thrill of speed and grew to love the danger it presented. But watching such crazy stunts on the track was hardly the best driving education for a young lad and, years later, it would be clear that racing had turned Shane into an irresponsible driver who was a menace on the public roads. He took many risks and, one day, was lucky to escape with his life – and Keith's – after pushing his luck too far.

As a boy, Shane longed to get behind the wheel of a car, but obviously he had a long time to wait before he was old enough to drive. So he managed to satisfy his urge for speed by riding bikes. He had loved riding bikes from his earliest years and, by the time he was seven, a new craze had taken grip across the world – BMX bike racing. The BMX is a specially designed bike which combines lightness with strength. The bike is light enough to ride fast and to be manouevred for difficult tricks, like wheelies, yet strong enough to withstand rough terrain and high jumps. The BMX phenomenon took hold in the early 1980s and it was perfect for Shane. From the age of seven, he was hooked on BMX bikes and quickly became a skilled rider who could perform many stunts. His natural love of speed and danger made him fearless and able to take greater risks than his friends and led to him becoming an excellent competitor on the competition circuit.

Shane became a respected rider in BMX rallies around Dublin and even in Portugal when he was on the annual family holiday. He raced on specially designed courses, which incorporated heavy bumps and high jumps, and became a mini celebrity who won several titles in various age groups. Shane would spend hours practising his skills and building up his stamina for races. When he wasn't riding his bike, or hanging out with his friends, he would be with his dad, either at the garage or at home as Brendan worked on the racing car. Shane was eager to learn about cars and would watch intently as his dad repaired the car's latest racing wounds. Shane loved the fact that the car looked a wreck on the outside with its dents and scratches, yet underneath the bonnet it concealed a powerful engine capable of beating a smart new road car.

Speed continued to be Shane's principal fascination throughout his childhood, and once he had grown out of BMX riding he moved on to the next logical stage to satisfy his obsession – motorbikes. He wasn't old enough to ride them on the roads, so he had to be content with letting the throttle out on private fields, where he was allowed to ride, or sneakily race around on the nearby beaches, or doing jumps over the bunkers on golf courses. Shane admits, 'We were little rogues when we were out on the bikes. As long as we were having fun, we didn't care if we messed up a golf course.'

While Shane's main interests were conventional for a boy, there was a quirky side to him, too. In particular, he had an odd fascination with the colour black. He had his own bedroom – one of the main advantages of having so many sisters – which gave him the chance to experiment with his own colour scheme. But, much to his mum's horror, Shane painted his bedroom walls black. Black is the worst possible colour to paint a room because it closes in the spaces and creates a gloomy, oppressive atmosphere, but Shane loved it and added to the spooky feel by hanging black drapes from the ceiling. Shane pursed his dark tastes further by dyeing his dark brown hair jet black, too. Another example of his odd side was his choice of pet. He bought a small South American snake which he called Caesar and kept in a box in his cupboard. He didn't tell his mum at first because she hates reptiles, so he had to feed it secretly on dead goldfish when she wasn't around.

Shane likes to be set aside from the gang and, years later when he was in Boyzone, he more than proved this by always being slightly different from the others. He created his own image by shaving a scar-like line through his right eyebrow and would always subtly alter a costume if the band were to appear in identical outfits. Basically, he would do anything that made him look more individual.

Although Shane strived to be different, unfortunately he was unavoidably typical of so many teenage boys when it came to school work: he was hopeless. He was too busy enjoying himself to worry about getting his homework done properly, or paying close attention in class, and was often in trouble for poor performance in lessons. He wasn't a bad or disruptive pupil, but simply uninterested and unmotivated. It wasn't even girls who were providing the distraction, as they do to so many teenage lads. In fact, Shane was very shy when he was a teenager, despite having so many sisters and such good looks.

'I was very shy and would never even have the guts to approach a girl in a disco to ask her to dance. I was told I was good looking, but that didn't give me loads of confidence. In fact, I didn't have time for girls because I was too busy with cars and riding bikes to be bothered. But I was bad at school because I was such a dreamer. I was in a complete day dream most of the time and at the end of one year, the head teacher called me in and said, "I think it is best if you don't come back next term." I said, "Why? I haven't done anything," and he said, "Precisely, Shane – you don't do *anything*." That was it – I had to leave, but I was really happy to go because I hated school,' says Shane.

When he left school at sixteen, Shane didn't have to think for too long or look too far for his first job; he became a trainee mechanic at his dad's garage. It seemed the natural and best solution to his future. Shane left school with no chance of carrying on to senior education to train for a more academically slanted career, so his options were limited. On the positive side, cars interested him more than anything and, in a way, he had already completed several years of training, thanks to his genuine passion for them. In many respects he was already qualified with a wide knowledge of mechanics, so he easily settled in to working at the garage. His dad was happy to have his son working alongside him. He knew garage work wouldn't win Shane worldwide acclaim, but it would provide him with a secure job, which was valuable in the competitive work environment for school leavers. Brendan was also pleased that he would be able to teach his son the business side of mechanics, so that maybe one day he could run his own garage. Shane was certainly pleased to be finished with school. He says, 'I loved working in the garage. I have always been into cars, so it was ideal for me. As far as I was concerned that was going to be my job for life. I had no idea then that I would end up doing something so different.'

Soon after turning seventeen in March 1993, Shane took his driving test and, as expected, passed first time. After all he'd spent many hours behind the wheel throughout his teenage years, and since working at the garage he had been allowed to drive cars around the forecourt and into the repair bays. In fact, Shane probably knew more about the mechanics of a car and how to handle them at speed than most examiners.

What the examiner couldn't know though, was just how stupidly Shane would drive once he had passed. As soon as he could drive legally, Shane did his best to do exactly the opposite, by driving illegally! Handing Shane the keys to a car with a free run of the Dublin roads was tantamount to giving a dehydrated alcoholic the keys to the drinks cabinet. Shane had been waiting for years to drive and he wasn't going to accept his new-found freedom by following the laws of the highway. His first instincts were to put his foot on the accelerator and keep pressing until it hit the floor. He says: 'As soon as my friends and I were seventeen we all got cars. We would drive around everywhere as fast as we could. I loved speed and going fast is natural to me. We got up to all kinds of crazy things. We would race around the back streets and sometimes we would drive into the country late at night. We would race with the lights off and you could barely see a thing. The driver who turned his lights back on first was the chicken. It was a daft game but it was great fun.'

Shane's first car was a jeep and he spent hours trying to make it go faster and look smarter. He would clean it lovingly and tune its engine, then thrash it to the limit of its capability. But it was his second car, an ageing Golf GTi, which became his first 'racing' car. It was black with a bright green stripe down either side and cost £1,500. The residents near Shane's house would grit their teeth in annoyance as they became familiar with the sound of the Golf's screeching tyres and loud music as he and his pals sped off like maniacs for a quick, top-speed spin in their cars.

Shane was pretty content with his life. He was doing a job he liked and was having a fun social life tearing around with his pals in their cars and going to nightclubs at weekends. He had a great deal of freedom and enough money in his pocket to allow him to do everything he wanted within reason. His parents were open minded and laid back about him going out, so there were no petty restrictions to make life awkward. He had a better time than many other seventeen-year-olds, so he had a lot to be grateful for. Shane would probably have been happy trundling along in that mode for many years if his best friend, Mark Walton, hadn't come to him with an idea which would dramatically change his life forever.

Mark had been close buddies with Shane since they were young boys. They rode BMX bikes together, hung around with the same crowd, went to the same parties, and now they raced around in their cars together. Mark was a talented Gaelic footballer who represented Ireland, but during one game, in Germany, he broke his ankle. It was the autumn of 1993 and the unfortunate accident would indirectly have an amazing impact on both their lives: it would lead to the formation of Boyzone.

Mark explains, 'I was the one who started Boyzone. It happened when I was stuck at home after breaking my ankle. I was off school and a couple of girls I knew knocked on the door and gave me a Take That video to watch. It was the band's first video, *Take That And Party*, and the girls told me to watch it because they thought I looked like Mark Owen. I wasn't really interested but when I watched the video I thought, "Wow, look at the lifestyles these guys are having."

'Right after that I told my mum and dad I was going to start the first Irish boy band. They laughed at me and thought it was a passing idea which I would forget about. I told my friends at school and everyone laughed at me. They thought I was crazy and didn't believe five Irish guys could make it in a boy band. But I knew it could work. I let them laugh and said, "You wait and see. This will happen and we'll be huge all over the world." I knew I would prove them wrong – I had total belief in the idea right from the start.

'I asked Shane if he wanted to be in a band. We had grown up together and are best friends. He also thought it was a bit far fetched, but was interested. He said, "Yeah why not, I'll give it a go."'

It was no wonder Shane was interested because he, too, had already been fascinated by the success of boy bands. When he was fourteen, he had seen the phenomenal rise of New Kids On The Block and was amazed how five average-looking guys could have such wild lives. Watching Donnie Wahlberg and his pals didn't have the same resounding impact as Bros had had on Ronan, or The Police on Mikey, but it had alerted Shane to a fantasy world that was remotely possible. The New Kids had long since burnt out, but Take That had already emerged from the ashes and Shane was well aware of the mania surrounding the Manchester group. Mark's idea was even more exciting because it had a novel twist: no boy band had ever come out of Ireland.

There was one major problem facing Mark and Shane: they lacked a hardened professional who could turn their dream into reality. Both New Kids On The Block and Take That had been cultivated by a guru figure within the music business. They didn't know anyone like that; but then someone told them about Louis Walsh.

6

CREATING BOYZONE

Louis Walsh was brought up on a farm in County Mayo, on the north-western coast of Ireland. He was the second child among seven brothers and two sisters. Despite his rural up-bringing, he had no desire to stay in the outer reaches of the country; Louis wanted to be in the thick of the action in a large city. The only place that offers a genuinely fast pace in Ireland is Dublin, so it wasn't long before he moved from home to the city. Louis, by his own admission, was a natural hustler, who had plenty of charm, quick wit and the gift of the gab. He found himself drawn to the music business and started out as a record plugger – the hard-selling job of getting radio stations to play new releases. It is a tough, and often thankless task, which requires plenty of determination and an extremely thick skin to shrug off endless rejections. Louis was perfect for the job and quickly built up a good reputation and contacts in the music world, before he eventually branched out into entertainment management. He secured himself some moderately successful Irish club acts and two artists who won the Eurovision Song Contest. But the bulk of Louis's clients were B-list entertainers working in second-rate venues on the club circuit. He wasn't happy. Louis was ambitious and he wanted a top-class international act.

Louis had seen the rise and fall of New Kids On The Block, followed by the success of Take That, and both groups convinced him that a similar style band should be started in Ireland. It was an idea he had harboured for some time, but it was all a question of timing and getting it up and running.

Mark Walton was told about Louis Walsh by a dancer he met at an audition for a show in Dublin. The lad had laughed about the idea, but said if anyone could help make it work, it was Louis. Mark fixed up a meeting and was thrilled with the response he got. Mark says, 'Louis was the only person who didn't laugh when I talked about my idea. He had thought about starting a band a while earlier, but had given up on the idea. He was really enthusiastic and told me to get someone else and come back and see him. I took Shane with me and we sang and danced for him. He said, "Great, you two can be the first members of the group." That's how it all started.'

The lads liked Louis's straight-talking, hard-nosed approach to the idea and Louis warmed to their raw belief and enthusiasm. They all clicked and began to plan how to get the other members of their embryonic supergroup. The first step was to organise open auditions to give all the untapped talent in Ireland a chance to try their luck at getting into the group. Louis arranged for a story about his quest to be broadcast on local television and commercial radio stations, as well as articles in the national tabloid newspapers. Shane and Mark appeared in interviews as the core members of the future group appealing for those with pop stardom ambitions to join them. Within hours of the story breaking, dozens of requests flooded into Louis's office from all over the country. The response was amazing and proved they were on to a good idea, showing that the public and the media felt the time was right for the talent from the Emerald Isle to show what they could do in the world of pop. Before the initial publicity splurge had finished, Louis had more than 300 applications. To filter through so many was a daunting task, but he felt confident that, if the necessary talent existed, then the pop stars of the future would be among the unknown lads in that pile of letters.

In the wake of the story, the prospect of becoming a star in the new supergroup became the topic of conversation in hundreds of homes. Ronan and Steve saw it as the big break they had been waiting for. Keith spotted Shane's picture in the paper and, naturally, fancied his chances, but he didn't apply in the normal route like the rest of the lads. Instead, he waited until he saw Shane at the gym one night and asked his friend to put a good word in for him with Louis.

Mikey was working at Annesley Motors when he heard Shane and Mark interviewed on the radio, and remembers the moment well. He says, 'I heard two of the lads who were already in the band talking about it. I knew I could do what they were doing, but I didn't take much notice because I thought there would be so many going for it. I got home that night and saw the story in the newspaper as well and my best friend said, "Go for it, you never know." I didn't think I stood a chance, but my dad coaxed me round as well, so I had a go.'

It took Louis, Mark and Shane several weeks to go through all the applications and decide on a format for the auditions. They chose the Ormond Centre in Dublin as the venue and planned to ask each hopeful to sing 'Careless Whisper', the moving ballad which George Michael had taken to No. 1 in August 1984. All the contenders would be videoed and judged on every aspect of their performance, from their singing, to their stage presence, character and, of course, their looks.

Louis was finally ready to hold the auditions in November 1993. Fittingly, Take That were going from strength to strength just as Boyzone were about to be formed. The Manchester group followed their No. 1 'Pray' with 'Relight My Fire', which also went straight to the top. It was the beginning of a British record-breaking string of chart-topping hits that would cement their position as *the* teen supergroup of the moment, if not the decade. Louis knew that Take That were red hot and untouchable. He was also acutely aware that he had yet to even find a few glowing embers to start his group, but he knew the flames of Take That's success would finally burn out as they had done for the New Kids. By then, he was confident the boys in his band would be more than ready to carry the torch of teen stardom.

One of the lads who joined the queue at the Ormond Centre was Richie Rock, the son of a well known Irish singer called Dickie Rock. Richie could play piano and had inherited a strong singing voice from his father. He would emerge as one of the lucky winners in the auditions, but, sadly, his dream of pop fame would turn into a nightmare of disappointment and bitterness. Richie got talking to Ronan and Steve as they waited to be called. Richie says, 'I didn't know them but we started chatting and got on well right away. It seemed ironic that out of all the lads there, we were drawn to each other. Everyone was really nervous about the auditions. We were called in separately and asked to sing "Careless Whisper". There was someone there to play the piano and a video camera was taping everything. Louis sat out front with two other guys. They all had pads of paper and were taking notes as each boy sang the song. You knew that the slightest thing wrong would be noted. It was a nerve-wracking atmosphere. My first audition went well and I was invited back.'

Louis had to be ruthless to get through so many hopefuls. He dismissed many simply on their looks, but most went because they didn't have good enough voices or any natural stage presence. He managed to whittle down the initial 300 to around fifty for the second audition which was held a week later. He spotted Ronan and Steve's natural talent immediately and put them near the top of his list. He felt sure they could form the backbone of the group because they had strong and very different voices, as well as good looks and a natural charm girls would adore. He was also impressed with Richie. Shane and Mark were allowed to sit out the early auditions because, as far as Louis was concerned, they were already in the group. Keith didn't attend the first audition and, if it hadn't been for an amazing coincidence, he may have even been considered for Boyzone.

'Shane didn't say a word to Louis after I met him at the gym, so nothing happened and I was pretty fed up,' Keith explains. 'A few weeks later, I was going mad dancing on the small stage at the POD nightclub when a guy came up to me and asked to have a chat. It was a bit weird. There are loads of homosexuals in that club and I was a bit worried about an older man trying to speak to me. I tried to ignore him but it turned out to be Louis. He said he liked the way I danced and asked me if I wanted to be in a pop group. He told me who he was and I couldn't believe it. We went out the back for a chat and I told him that I knew Shane and that I had wanted to meet him for ages. He interviewed me that night and we got on really well. He invited me down to the second audition and, if it hadn't been for that coincidence, I may never have been involved with Boyzone. I had to sing and dance for them at the audition and I was scared stupid.'

For the second test, all the lads had to sing two songs to a backing tape. They could choose one of the songs; Mikey selected the stirring love song, 'Two Out Of Three Ain't Bad' by Meat Loaf, which he felt would show the wide range of his voice; Keith chose 'I'm Too Sexy', the song he had stripped to at the hen night because it gave him a chance to show off his dance rhythm. Ronan decided to sing 'Father and Son', the song he had loved since he was a young boy, and Richie chose Elton John's 'Your Song'. He particularly impressed Louis by playing the piano to that song.

The task of picking the best all-round talent became harder, but Louis managed to trim it down to ten, who were invited back for a third and final audition. Shane and Mark had to take part in the last audition, on a Thursday night, to prove they were capable of performing as well as the others.

Louis had such difficulty choosing between the remaining boys that he decided to make the group a six-piece. He selected Ronan, Steve, Shane, Mark, Keith and Richie Rock after that final audition. By coincidence, all, except Richie, were from the Northside of Dublin. Mikey was among the four who were turned down, but he was philosophical about the rejection. He says, 'I was disappointed not to be chosen after getting so far, but I didn't get too upset. I knew deep down that something would happen for me later.'

It would be many months before Mikey would get his big break, but his self-belief would prove to be justified.

Louis was happy with his choices. 'You need working-class guys because they want material things, like nice clothes and cars. There's a hunger there and they don't mind working for it. I'm from a working-class background, so I have that same hunger. I was also looking for the right attitude. They had to really *want* to be pop stars. There were a lot of good-looking boys at the auditions who could sing well, but couldn't dance or weren't hungry enough to make it. When Stephen and Ronan sang I just couldn't believe it; they had star quality all over their faces and I knew I had two great singers there. The next step was to get some other guys to fit in around them.'

The lads who were chosen that night were ecstatic and were quickly given a glimpse of the exciting times that lay ahead. They were whisked off to celebrate at the POD nightclub, where there was a fashion show being staged. It was a night that Richie will never forget: 'There was a great atmosphere among us boys. It had been a worrying few weeks trying to get into the group and suddenly it had happened – we were in. We were taken down to the club and that was where I got my first taste of what it must be like to be in a pop band. We were taken straight past the queue into the club and people were buying us drinks. There was some press there for the fashion show and they took our picture. Everyone seemed to know about the search for the band – it was almost as if we were famous already. I thought, "If it's like this now, what will it be like in the future?" It was a fantastic feeling – I felt like I was walking on air and we all had such high hopes.'

If the nightclub celebration was exciting, it was nothing compared to what happened the next night. Louis arranged for all six to go on *The Late, Late Show* – Ireland's most popular live chat show, hosted by Gaye Byrne. They were interviewed and performed one hastily arranged dance routine while miming to the backing tape of the song 'Burn Baby Burn'. Unfortunately, they had only been given a few hours to rehearse and that was nowhere near long enough. The lads barely knew one another, let alone how to perform like a slickly choreographed pop group on live national television. They looked amateurish and out of their depth, and the experience left them feeling dejected. They feared they had blown their big chance before they had even started and their worries were compounded when they read scathing criticism in the papers following that performance. Certain sections of the Irish media were appalled at Boyzone's début appearance and were quick to write them off as an untalented bunch of lads who were the product of a cynical marketing exercise. The stinging reports, which came so soon after the exhilaration of their success in the auditions, brought the lads back to earth with a nasty bump. It was a swift and harsh lesson, but it did them the world of good.

It made them realise just how much work they needed to do before they could be transformed from everyday Northside lads into genuine pop stars who could captivate an audience and sell records around the world.

7

TERROR ON THE ROAD

It was all very well for Ronan to lap up the glory of his triumph in the auditions, but he was forgetting one big problem he had yet to solve: he was still at school. He was only sixteen, which was hardly the ideal age to throw in your education for the wild notion of becoming a pop star. His parents were pleased he had been picked for Boyzone, but the fact that he would have to leave school to continue with the band put a different complexion on the matter. They weren't impressed with the idea, and neither were his teachers, so Ronan was faced with some severe opposition. The main stumbling block was Ronan's running career and the university scholarship he had been offered in America. It was a fantastic opportunity that would change his life. The experience had been good for his brother Gerard. Although Gerard hadn't pursued his athletics much further on the international scene, he had settled in New York and was having a great time in America. Going to university there was Ronan's chance to break away from Dublin and make something of his life. His parents and his running coach still believed he had a realistic chance of becoming a national athletics hero. How on earth could he throw all that away on some daft pipe dream of pop stardom?

Ronan was in a dilemma, too. He desperately wanted to go to America and understood his parents reservations about Boyzone. He was aware that although Louis Walsh believed the band would make it, there were no guarantees. Sure, Take That and New Kids On The Block were success stories, but how many similar dreams had been

45

left in tatters in the shadow of those two success stories? Bad Boys Inc and Worlds Apart were two recent examples of groups which had been formed with all the promise of chart success, only to vanish after a year or more of hard slog, with barely a top-ten hit to their credit. It could all go disastrously wrong for Boyzone, too, and could even fizzle out within a few months. By then, Ronan's chance of going to university would be gone and his bright athletics future would have stalled on the blocks. He would have to pick up the pieces and find something else to do with the added worry of having no academic qualifications. Ronan knew for sure he had no interest in school and that he would only stay there to secure good enough grades to go to the States. If it came to a choice, he knew he wanted to be a singer more than a runner. But it was a horrendously hard decision for such a young lad to make, and the reaction to Boyzone following *The Late, Late Show* had hardly inspired confidence.

He sought advice from his sister, Linda, who also lived in New York. Ronan says, 'My mum was dead against me joining the band. She said, "There's no way you're giving up school." All the teachers told me that my education had to come first and that I was wasting my time singing. But all I wanted to do was get out of school. I had a chat with my sister and she convinced me to go for it. She told me that if it all went badly wrong I could always go back to night-school and study later. She agreed that joining the band was a once in a lifetime chance, which I may regret not taking. I made the decision to leave school and it was more or less without my mum's approval. My parents had a good chat with the head teacher. They all knew I couldn't concentrate on school work, so they let me go. I was so pleased to leave.

'I wasn't so happy about giving up running and I tried to keep it going when we started the group, but I was eating badly and going to bed late. My fitness went downhill very quickly. I like to think I could have got an Olympic medal eventually, but athletics takes a lot of time and you have to be totally dedicated. You have to devote your life to it and be in peak condition the whole time. That means eating the right things, taking vitamins and getting lots of sleep. You have to train twice a day and have so much determination. When it came to it, I didn't have all that it takes – I wanted to be in the band more.

I would definitely have made my mark in Ireland, but running is a one-man game and I loved the thought of being in a team.'

Louis knew there would be family resistance from the other parents too, so he went to meet them to explain his strategy for turning their sons into stars. He only wanted the lads involved if they had the complete backing of their families, so the meetings were essential to the whole Boyzone idea. He appreciated the boys were taking enormous risks with their futures, but he was adamant it could work and was an educated gamble, not just a hopeless long shot. He had many powerful contacts in the music business who would give the boys the best chance of cracking it. Louis helped to persuade the parents of his commitment to making it a success by telling them that he was staking every penny he possessed on the project. Louis had always been a good talker and he managed to placate even the most cynical of them. Keith's mum and dad, in particular, were against the idea. Keith had done well in his first year of the architecture course, but quit to join Boyzone. His mum was upset he was throwing away a solid and promising career on such a crazy dream and his dad also came down heavily on his son when he started drawing unemployment benefit after leaving college. Patricia Duffy says: 'I was shocked he wanted to join a band while he was doing so well at architecture. He told me about the auditions but I didn't pay much attention. He missed the first one and I was delighted because I thought he might settle down and forget about it, but he didn't. I was dead against the whole thing. The music business is such an odd world, with so many temptations. I couldn't help but worry where it would lead.'

Keith adds: 'My parents went crazy and it was very difficult convincing them that it was the right thing. They wanted me to get a proper job and have a secure future. They thought I was throwing everything away and would end up a down and out. My dad was very tough on me and he hated it when I was on the dole. He would give me lectures that he wouldn't tolerate having a son who did nothing all day. We had a lot of rows, but I knew I was doing the right thing.'

All the parents finally accepted their sons' decisions, and then Louis made sure they all took individual legal advice before signing their contract with him. He didn't want any problems in the future and wanted a clear conscience that Ronan and the others knew exactly what they were getting involved in. Once all the paper work was settled, it was time for the lads to go to work and start learning to become pop stars.

They were left very much to their own devices during the first few months of 1994. They had vocal training and Louis instructed them to prepare a short and slick gig which they could perform at small clubs in Dublin and in provincial theatres. A series of low profile appearances would be their training ground. The lads met as often as possible to work out dance routines and choose songs they could cover. It was a difficult time. They weren't given any professional help, so they could only be guided by their own instincts and any ideas they could borrow by watching other teen bands. Louis wanted to be with them, but his priority rested with the business side of the venture. He felt it was good for the boys to work things out for themselves because at least that way they would create an identity of their own. If producers and others hardened music people were brought in right at the start, the true characters of the lads would be submerged and they would just develop into automaton performers with no charisma. There would be plenty of time for the professionals to fine-tune their act later.

Louis's main concern was getting the record companies interested, so, in those early months, he set out to sell the idea of Boyzone to the men with the money and the power to make it all happen. He went armed with a photo of his group and a short demo tape, which is a standard requirement to promote a new band. Louis was relying on other powerful reinforcements in his armoury, like his quit wit and charm, not to mention his tenacity, to win the battle with the record companies. They are notoriously tough companies to deal with and Louis wasn't surprised when his early approaches drew a blank. He wasn't the first manager to go knocking at the door of the record companies with the promise that his band were the next Take That, and nor would he be the last. The rejection letters began to pile up and Louis had to accept that securing a record deal would be harder than he had initially hoped.

The problems with the record companies were bad enough, but

Louis was faced with a more serious worry when he heard about a serious car accident Shane and Keith had been involved in. Shane had continued to drive like a lunatic and late one night, when he was going home after a practise session with Boyzone, he pushed his luck too far. Shane was driving his black Golf GTi and dropped Ronan off first, then headed for Donaghmede with Keith in the passenger seat.

It was around 1 am. The roads were quiet, but they were slightly wet from some earlier rain. The tyres on the Golf were also wearing thin from months of hard driving. As usual, Shane liked to put his foot down when the way was clear and soon he was doing 110mph. As he approached a bend he slowed down to 90 mph, but he was going too fast and couldn't break hard without skidding. The terror of the next few seconds will always stay with Keith. 'Shane was driving like a complete maniac. He was going far too fast for the bend and the back wheels slid away as we turned. I knew we weren't going to make it, so I braced myself. Shane lost control and I thought we were going to die,' says Keith.

A wheel hit the kerb and the car flipped into the air and began somersaulting down the road. Inside, Shane and Keith curled up and clung on desperately. The car continued rolling for what seemed and age and finally stopped on its roof.

'If we hadn't been wearing seat belts we would have been finished,' Keith claims. 'I was left dangling upside down from my safety belt. I knew I was okay, but I was too scared to open my eyes or speak because I couldn't hear a sound from Shane. I felt sure if I looked at him I would see him all broken up and dead. I still had my eyes closed when I heard Shane say, "You all right?" It was such a relief. I groaned, "Yeah," and then, cool as you like, Shane said, "We might as well get out now," as if he had just parked the car normally, not rolled it over!

'Once we crawled out I was shaking and really nervous. Shane was fine. He had a baseball bat in the boot and he started hitting the car with it and laughing like crazy. I think he's slightly mad, a bit touched. I must admit I started laughing as well after a while, but more out of relief than anything else. I couldn't believe the state of the car. It was on the other side of the road, a long way from the bend, and was a total right-off. All the windows were smashed and the bodywork was battered. The roof had been completely crushed over the driver's head. I think twice before I get in a car with Shane these days, and I still have the pain from my injuries.'

Shane laughs when he recalls the accident. 'I get an amazing rush of adrenalin when I go fast. I love the buzz the fear gives me, but I pushed it too far that night. Thankfully, I always drive with the seat well reclined. If I hadn't been in that position that night, my head would have been taken clean off. If Keith and I hadn't walked away from that crash, who knows what would have happened to Boyzone? I was fine and not shaken up at all. If anything, I got a real buzz out of it, but Keith was a bit scared. We have had very different upbringings which is why we reacted differently. I used to watch my dad stock-car racing when I was a kid and I saw drivers crawl out of the most terrible crashes. Racing cars, speed and crashing has been part of my life. For me, crashing is good if no one gets hurt and you don't hit another car. The Golf was only worth about £1,500, so it was no great loss. I love the buzz I get from pushing a car to the limit. I know driving like that is dangerous and people must think I'm a nutter, but I only drive fast at night when the roads are clear and there's no danger of going into other cars.'

Whatever Shane's excuses, Louis wasn't interested. He was appalled he could be so irresponsible. Louis was aware none of the lads were innocent angels, but, now they were involved in a serious business, he expected them to behave more maturely. He was staking every penny he had on their future, so the last thing he wanted was for one of them to get injured in an accident that was down to their stupidity. He gave all the lads a stern talking to and drew up legally binding contracts which restricted their activities. The agreement included a ban on them taking part in physical contact sports, such as football and hurling, as well as boozing and taking drugs. Louis knew that if they wanted to make it, they had to stay fit and healthy. The agreement also made the lads promise to keep any girlfriends secret.

Although the contracts solved certain tangible problems with the boys' behaviour, they wouldn't help cure more complicated worries that were beginning to emerge with Mark and Richie. The journey to get Boyzone on the road wouldn't prove to be as smooth as Louis had hoped, and, sadly, there would be some casualties along the way.

8

LEAVING FOR A REASON

The first few months of 1994 tested the spirits of all six lads to the limit. They were expected to work week after week with few signs of encouragement to spur them on. They hoped Louis would secure a quick record deal through his good contacts, but nothing materialised and there seemed little hope that anything was going to happen in the near future. Louis was certainly fulfilling one promise – spending money on the band. He brought in top choreographer Vennol John, who had worked with Kylie Minogue and Madonna, to develop some quality dance routines; he secured the services of writer Ray Hedges and producer Ian Levine who had helped New Kids On The Block; Louis also hired a slick London-based PR company headed by Liz Watson whose brief was to create some hype about Boyzone in the key teen magazines and tabloid newspapers in Ireland and the UK. Louis then paid for the boys to have a full session with a stylist and a top photographer, so the band's image could be sharpened. On top of this, he rented an expensive studio for them to record another demo tape. They sang 'Can You Feel It', the dance song The Jacksons took into the top-ten in 1981. Louis felt the tape and the well-styled pictures would help him sell the band to a record label. He hit the streets to continue banging on the doors of the record companies, but he was soon faced with rejection or silence. He says, 'I tried every record company but they all said no. A lot of them didn't even bother getting back to me.'

The pressure was mounting and none more so than on Louis's

finances. His personal resources had been drained by his investments in Boyzone and, around March 1994, he had to concede that he needed an injection of cash if he was to continue giving the band a fair shot at making it. He approached his good friend John Reynolds, the wealthy owner of the POD nightclub in Dublin, and convinced him to become the band's co-manager. Louis and John set up the WAR company (Walsh and Reynolds) which would manage Boyzone. They agreed that Louis would be responsible for the running of the group, while John would focus on the business side. John handed over a five-figure sum to keep everything going.

While Louis's immediate cash flow problems were solved, the lads themselves were feeling pressures of their own. The uncertainty of getting a record deal had rattled their confidence and their worries were compounded by negative rumblings from their friends and families. Everyone seemed to think they were chasing a pipe dream. Keith, in particular, was having regular rows with his father, who was appalled that his son was drawing the dole while, as he saw it, dreaming his life away on some pop fantasy. Ronan and Steve only managed to keep their families content by working part-time in shops in the centre of Dublin, so at least they were earning their own pocket money, Ronan at Korky's shoe shop and Steve at Makullas clothes shop. Shane paid his way at home by working at his dad's garage, so things weren't too bad for him. It was Richie and Mark who were having real problems.

Richie was the most despondent and wasn't afraid to say it. He had become impatient with Boyzone's lack of progress. He was used to seeing action in the music business after watching his father's successful career and he expected results. Richie wasn't content to meander along waiting for a record deal, and his commitment to the band began to suffer. He was sick of not having any money in his pocket, so he skipped rehearsals and a few early gigs to work as a DJ in nightclubs. According to Richie, there was also a personality clash between him and John Reynolds, which made his position in the group more awkward.

The pressure of fame was already taking its toll on Mark. Even though Boyzone had yet to release their first single, they already had many fans. The hype in the media over the search for Ireland's first boy band had secured a loyal following and even in those early months, girls waited outside the boys' homes. Unfortunately, Mark was finding his taste of fame rather bitter.

'I found it really tough in those first few months,' he says. 'Shane and I were the first guys in the band, so we had lots of fans right from the start and long before we even had a record out. I found it really hard to cope. I had to go on radio and on big television shows and was on the front pages of newspapers. It was all such a shock. I had loads of girls outside my house and phoning me all night. I didn't know how to deal with it and felt embarrassed and couldn't relax with them. When I was performing with Boyzone I kept thinking, "Is this me? Am I doing the right thing?"

'To be honest, I simply couldn't handle it. I was so young and, looking back, I was suffering from a complete lack of confidence. It was a strange thing for me to be doing. I had done a bit of modelling before that but I had never been into music in a big way. Suddenly I was in a hot teen group. It was all such a change that I got very worried.

'I was with Boyzone for nine months and the pressure built up on me as we got nearer to launching the first single. We all knew something wasn't right. I was totally committed to the band, but the other guys sensed I wasn't happy, and Louis knew for sure there were problems, too.

'Everything got on top of me. I was still at school, but I was taking loads of time off for Boyzone and I was worried I was throwing my education away. I feared that if things didn't work out I would end up on the dole because I had no qualifications. At the time my grandfather was dying and my mum was ill. Maybe I was being a softie, but there were so many emotions going through my head.

'In the end, it all got too much and one night I was laying in bed crying my eyes out. I was scared of the future. I knew I had to get my life sorted out and make sure I was on the right road, or I would end up very unhappy and depressed. That night I decided to leave Boyzone. I told Louis and when I saw the lads, they were upset. Ronan and Steve said, "Oh my God, are you sure?" I chatted to Shane for a few hours. He didn't want me to leave because we had started it together and we are best friends, but I had made up my mind. I was relieved once I had made the decision.'

It was a blow to lose Mark. It had been his foresight and vision which had started everything, so it was sad he couldn't continue. But, from an objective view of the band, it wasn't a disaster. Who had ever heard of a six-piece boy band? Five was the traditional figure and, with Mark gone, it may even provide the key to a record deal. Although the numerical balance was now right, there were more deep-rooted problems which would bubble to the surface soon after Mark's departure, and it would spell the end of another lad's dream of stardom.

The band had started to perform short gigs at clubs in Dublin and major towns on the outskirts of the city to build up their profile. They were vital appearances to generate much needed publicity for the band, but, more importantly, Louis invited record company scouts to watch, so it was crucial the lads made a solid, professional impression. Unfortunately, the gigs could only be done successfully with lots of practise, but they all came at a time when Richie's interest was hitting rock bottom. He became unreliable.

'It was really tough in the beginning,' Richie explains. 'We were left on our own a lot and we hardly had any contact from Louis. It seemed like nothing was happening, yet we were still expected to meet up and practise. From the beginning, Louis always expected me to organise everyone. I had to ring all the lads and arrange when and where to meet. We were all getting disillusioned, but it seemed to affect me more than the others. I was fed up working in the band when I didn't have a penny in my pocket. I started not turning up at meetings because I couldn't see the point of going somewhere unless something positive was happening with the band. But Louis got really angry. I told him I wasn't happy but he wasn't interested in my complaints. He just told me to do what he said.

'Things got worse and there was always a bad atmosphere between me and Louis. The last straw came when we were due to do a gig at The Rock Garden nightclub at 11 pm. Louis called me at about 8 pm and told me to ring all the lads to make sure they all knew what time to be at the club. I then started to watch a film on television. It was *A League of Their Own*, with Madonna, which was being shown twice in one night on a satellite channel. I fell asleep and woke up at 11.15 pm. The film was still on, but it was the second showing. I panicked

Ronan celebrates the MTV award.

The boys look like cool veterans of teen pop in their designer outfits.

Peter Andre joins in the celebrations at the MTV Awards.

Keith during a show in 1996.

The boys don't need fur coats to make them a hot act on stage.

Shane is ready for combat during one tour.

Ronan is now a bigger star than his childhood heroes, Bros.

Steve catches up on the latest chart news while the others prepare for a TV interview.

Long-haired Ronan
looking jaded and moody.

Mark Walton, the boy
who dreamed up Ireland's
answer to Take That.

Now Mark (at the back) is ready for stardom with Only Us.

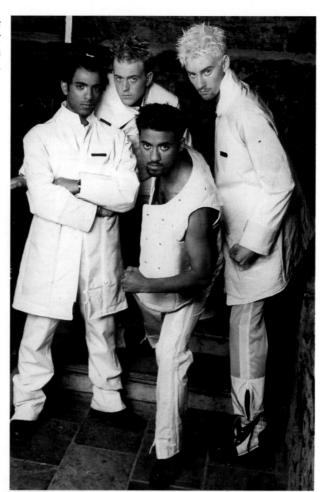

The original six piece line-up of Boyzone with Richie Rock (first from the left) and Mark Walton (behind Ronan). (Courtesy: *Daily Star*, Ireland)

Shane and Keith walked away from the wreckage of this Golf.

Dressed to thrill in black, Boyzone sing tracks from 'A Different Beat'.

and got down to the club as soon as I could, but I had missed the whole gig.

'When I got there, Louis came up to me and went mad. He started screaming and shouting at the top of his voice. He was calling me names and telling me I was unreliable and a compulsive liar. I didn't get a chance to say a word because he wouldn't stop shouting. I was so angry with myself because I had wanted to be there. I had organised the others and made sure they went to the gig. If only I hadn't laid down to watch that film, I wouldn't have gone to sleep. While Louis was ranting, John Reynolds was standing there gloating and loving every minute of it. Louis said I was finished and that he never wanted to see me again. All this happened with loads of people watching. It was like the music had stopped and everyone was looking at me – it was terrible. When Louis stopped, Keith came up to me. He had tears in his eyes and told me it would be all right once Louis had calmed down. But it never was OK again – I was out of the band from that moment. I was really upset and went out and got seriously drunk. The hardest thing to take is knowing that if I had stuck with it just a little bit longer, I would have made it with the others.'

But it wasn't to be. Richie was out and nothing would change Louis's mind. As far as he was concerned, he had given Richie more than enough chances and there simply wasn't room for someone who wasn't totally committed. Louis realised it was tough for the lads to maintain their belief in him while nothing tangible was happening, but they had to stay strong, otherwise everything would fall apart. Louis was slogging his heart out trying to get Boyzone a record deal, so the last thing he needed was a member of the group not showing up for an important gig which could be vital to their future. It had been bad enough losing Mark, but at least he had been surplus to requirements. Now Louis needed a quick replacement for Richie. Luckily, he had several reserves from that final audition who could easily fill the vacancy, and Mikey Graham was top of that list.

Mikey had continued working as a mechanic and was delighted to get the phone call from Louis. Mikey is a level-headed young man with a cool attitude to life. He hadn't sunk into a deep depression since losing out and, although he was thrilled to join Boyzone, he wasn't the type to get carried away. He was ready to put in all the work and do everything he was told to do. He was reliable, industrious and got on well with the other lads. Louis welcomed Mikey's mature approach and breathed a sigh of relief. Mikey was older than the others and had a serious side which Louis felt would help keep Boyzone steady.

Richie Rock had salt rubbed into his wounds soon after his departure when he heard that Boyzone had secured a record contract. After months of hustling, Louis finally pulled off a deal with Paul Keogh, the managing director of Polygram Ireland. He liked their style and sound, and felt they had the necessary raw talent that could be nurtured once they had established themselves. Keogh believed the time was right for another boy band to start out and be ready to succeed Take That once they had peaked. He also felt that the novelty of being the first pop group of its kind to originate from Ireland would be an added attraction which would give them the edge over other pretenders to the pop throne.

The contract was for three singles with an option to release an album should the singles do well. It was a good deal and one that everyone was relieved to sign. It had been a worrying six months since the band had been formed in November and, at times, even Louis's optimism had been shaken. He had received numerous rejections from record companies in Ireland and the UK, and many hadn't even bothered to return his calls or answer his letters. But, almost at the eleventh hour he had pulled off a deal with one of the major players in the music business. If anyone could break Boyzone in Ireland, Polygram could.

The speed of Boyzone's launch, and subsequent take off into superstardom, was breathtaking, even by the crazy standards of the pop music world. Within a month, they had chosen their début single, recorded it and even shot the promotional video. The song they chose was a cover version of The Detroit Spinners' classic 'Working My Way Back To You', which had given the American group its only UK No. 1 in 1980. Mikey and Steve shared the vocals, and Ronan sang 'Father And Son' on the B-side.

The Irish public had been waiting to hear what had happened to the Dublin lads who had won the national hunt for a boy band and they got the answer when Boyzone were launched in a blaze of publicity. The group returned to appear on Gaye Byrne's *The Late, Late Show*, the scene of their shambolic, and depressing first performance. Back then, they had been six raw, local lads who were still giddy from winning the auditions when they were paraded on TV. One minute they were nobodies, the next they were expected to perform on Ireland's biggest showbiz talk show. It had been a nerve-wracking disaster, but the second visit couldn't have been more different. Boyzone were now five well-groomed and confident young stars in the making. They were relaxed and charming and they performed their single with slick professionalism. The lads looked cool in their trendy new clothes, they danced well and the song sounded good. All those months of hard slog in the dance studio had paid off. The transformation was incredible, and Gaye Byrne and his audience were amazed.

Pop fans were impressed too, and within a few weeks 'Working My Way Back To You' went to No. 3 in the Irish charts. It was a stunning success for a first single which Ronan and the boys, Louis Walsh and John Reynolds toasted with champagne, as well as a few pints of Guinness, Ireland's favourite beer. The lads from nowhere had arrived.

From the moment 'Working My Way Back To You' was a hit, the lives of all five lads were changed forever. They had dreamed of being famous for so many years and now it was all about to come true in the most spectacular way. The term 'overnight fame' is a clichéd expression, but it's appropriate with Boyzone's success. Most bands takes year to break into the big time and need to release a couple of singles before they secure a hit. Everything happened instantly for Boyzone and they have never looked back.

They all had to give up their jobs as they were caught up in a whirl of publicity and promotion which took them all over Ireland. They appeared on countless television programmes and radio road shows, and won over an army of fans with live performances at summer music festivals and signing sessions in record shops. One of the highlights of that summer was appearing alongside the heroic Irish national soccer team on their return from the World Cup in America.

Boyzone were cheered by more than 60,000 in Dublin centre – and almost stole the show from the footballers.

Once the promotion work in Ireland was finished, the band flew to London for a series of public appearances and short gigs to build their fan base in the UK and to record the next single. While in London they also recorded 'Love Me For A Reason', which had been a No. 1 hit for the American pop phenomenon The Osmonds, twenty years earlier. Even two decades had not eroded the charm of the ballad and it cast its spell again to help launch Boyzone in Britain and Europe. It went straight to No. 1 in Ireland and confirmed Boyzone mania across the Emerald Isle. The boys could no longer walk down the street or go shopping in Dublin without being mobbed. Fans traced their homes and waited outside for hours on end hoping for a glimpse of their heroes.

The success of 'Love Me For A Reason' secured Boyzone a record deal in the UK, so, after dominating the Irish charts all summer, they headed to Britain for the winter. The key to their success there was the *Smash Hits* Roadshow. *Smash Hits* is Britain's biggest and most influential teen magazine and each year it hosts a series of live pop shows with established favourites and the best of the newcomers. The roadshow culminates in the Poll Winners' Party in London, which is broadcast live on television. The highlight of the show is the results of the *Smash Hits* readers' survey. Boyzone had emerged as the clear stars of the roadshow and were voted 'Best Band On The Road'. It was a tremendous accolade and the lads collected their award in front of 25,000 hysterical girls in the arena, plus 11 million people watching on television.

Success in the poll was followed by their first cover of *Smash Hits* and then 'Love Me For A Reason' was released in December. It climbed to No. 2 and only missed the No. 1 spot because of East 17's 'Stay Another Day'. But Boyzone had no complaints. They had started 1994 full of hope and it had ended with incredible triumph. In just over twelve months they had risen from everyday jobs and anonymity among the masses of Dublin's Northside, to be pop stars with two hit records and thousands of fans screaming for them. If they had achieved all that in such a short time, what more could they do in the future?

9

UNLOCKING THE FUTURE

On Saturday 21 January 1995, I was the first writer to interview Boyzone at their homes in Dublin. 'Love Me For A Reason' had dominated the charts on both sides of the Irish Sea for many weeks and Boyzone were being hailed as the next teen sensations. The lads had enjoyed a whirlwind six months since their launch. Their faces were staring from posters on thousands of bedroom walls and their music was being played in a dozen or more countries. Yet the glamorous, sex symbol public image of the band was a far cry from the characters of the young men I met that day. The first visit was to Ronan's house in the Swords area. As the two of us sat in the lounge chatting, it was hard to imagine that this fresh-faced seventeen-year-old, in jeans and a sweatshirt, had become such a heart-throb to so many. It was something Ronan, too, was finding hard to accept. He talked about his early days, his athletics success, and how he worshipped Bros. He was the first to admit he had never even had a serious girlfriend, but now he was the target of mass adulation. What had happened to Bros was now happening to him. In his bedroom Ronan still had the treasured blue electric guitar which had signalled the start of his passion for music, and weaving its way across the floor was his Scalextric. It looked like the typical bedroom of any teenage lad, yet this was Ronan Keating, pop star and teen idol.

'I can't believe all this has happened to me,' he said. 'A little while ago, girls wouldn't have looked at me twice if I was walking down the street. Now they are writing to me and going crazy whenever they see me. The feeling it gives you is difficult to explain because it feels so unreal, but it's great and we all love it. I'm not letting it go to my head because it can turn you into an egomaniac. It has been fantastic and we hope this is just the start. The buzz I get from being on stage in front of thousands of people sends shivers up my spine. It is amazing, but we have to realise that all this doesn't last long.'

Mikey was typically laid back when we met at his house in Coolock. He still had the same bedroom, but he no longer had to share it with Niall. It was a tiny box-room, with barely enough space for a single bed, a chest of drawers and his keyboard in the corner. He talked fondly of those days when the family would lie in bed filling the house with singing. Now, like his hero Sting, Mikey's voice was entertaining an army of fans, but he was taking it all in his stride and remaining level-headed.

'Personally, I don't see myself as a pop star,' he said. 'That's what we are called, but I'm no different and I have no trouble coasting between my life in Ireland and my life in the group. They are two different worlds, but I'm pretty stable and there is no egomania in either. I am still the same as before we made any records and I don't think any of us will change. The people who change are generally the ones who believe in their own publicity. We all know that publicity is a smokescreen. We also know that you can be here one minute in this business, and gone the next. I don't want to sound pessimistic, but we are aware that Boyzone won't last forever, so we will enjoy it while we can. Hopefully, we won't be finished for a long time, but, if it ends, we will accept it graciously.

'The market was ready for something new and basically we have been the only new band around. One of the major things that has helped us in the UK is the novelty of being Irish. Almost everyone in Ireland has relatives in England, so the word spread pretty quickly. People seem to love the Irish, because we come across as people who like having a good time.

'It sounds strange, but I felt my life has always been heading towards this. I come from a musical family and I always wanted to make a living out of music, so it didn't come to me as a big surprise. The only thing that has surprised me is how fast it happened. We were psyching ourselves up for a long slog because it normally takes a lot of bands years to break through, but we seem to have got there in a matter of months – it's unbelievable. Our lives are changing every day. I had to give up my job, but there was no crying about that. I get noticed in the streets now and kids come knocking at the door. I was a bit frightened of the fans at first and wondered how it would change my life, but it's not too bad yet. I think the fans in the UK can be more forward, but the kids from my area in Dublin won't go beyond a certain mark, so I think it is a bit easier being a pop star in Ireland than in England.

At Shane's house in Donaghmede, four or five young girls were waiting outside. Shane grinned widely as he signed autographs. He had longed for that kind of attention since he saw the rise of New Kids On The Block five years earlier. Like Ronan and Mikey, Shane was just as you would expect any normal young man: easy going with a laddish glint in his eye, as if he can't really believe his luck. Clearly, there are odd quirks in Shane that make him stand out from the crowd. His partly-shaved right eyebrow certainly looks odd up close and then there's the fascination for the colour black. His bedroom walls are painted black and dark drapes billow from the ceiling. He also shows great affection for his pet snake, Caesar. Apart from these slight eccentricities, Shane is friendly and sincere. Slumping into the settee in the conservatory at the back of the house, he was nonchalant as he considered his new-found fame. 'I don't think of myself as an idol or anything,' he said. 'I'm still very down-to-earth. I'm amazed I'm doing this because I have always been very shy, so I never thought I could get up on stage in front of so many people. It seems odd having fans outside the house waiting for me, but it's very exciting and I wouldn't change things for a minute. It's great fun.'

Keith and Steve couldn't have been more different. Keith is full of confidence and barely pauses for breath when he talks. In fact, he sometimes talks so fast, and with such a strong Irish accent, that is hard to understand him. In complete contrast, Steve is physically half the size of Keith and twice as quiet. He appears painfully shy, but, under that meek exterior lies a determined and ambitious young man. Love-struck fans were waiting outside his house, too, and when I asked him if he was worried about the loss of his privacy and being followed everywhere, he answered without needing time to think.

'No, this is what I want,' he said confidently, with his trademark wide smile.

Boyzone were certainly enjoying their new-found fame. They were mobbed everywhere, and lapped up the screaming hysteria which punctuated every public appearance. But it was also a time for worry. They had secured two hits and were the band of the moment, but certain sections of the music media were still criticising their success. Basically, Boyzone weren't credible and had achieved too much, too quickly. Their ascent was shrugged off as lucky and won on the back of skilled marketing and other artists' songs, not on the merit of their own ability. This negative reaction was an ugly smudge on what had been a beautiful canvas for Ronan and the group. They desperately wanted it erased. The only way to silence their critics and win their respect was to write their own material. Cover versions had always been a safe bet to make a good start in the music business, but it wasn't a route that would provide longevity.

Ronan, Mikey and Steve had been working together on original songs since the earliest days of Boyzone. All three had spent years writing songs on their own before the group formed and Mikey had already completed fifty-five. It was a natural step for them to begin composing together. They were all eager to prove their song-writing talent, so they were horrified when their record company bosses said they wanted the band to release another cover version for the third single. The executives were certain it was the simplest and safest way to secure another hit to build on Boyzone's success. They didn't want to risk all the hard work the lads had done by releasing an original song from young and untested pop stars. The boys, however, saw it very differently. They had been appalled by the criticism they had received and were determined to prove they were capable of composing a hit. 'We wanted to release one of our own songs, which would shut up the begrudgers,' says Ronan.

One song the boys favoured was called 'Key To My Life', which Ronan, Mikey and Steve had written the previous summer. It was a moving ballad with lyrics based on their childhood infatuations for schoolteachers. The record company bosses were impressed with the song and were quickly convinced it was worth releasing in preference to a track pulled from the archives of past hits. The decision came with a certain degree of risk for Boyzone. If 'Key To My Life' was a hit, then they were guaranteed an extension to their recording contract, which would see the release of their first album and several more singles. If it was a flop, the future of the band would be reconsidered and it was just possible it would signal the end. 'It's a risk bringing out an original, but it's a good song and the fans will love it,' predicted Mikey confidently.

And he was right. 'Key To My Life' went to No. 1 in Ireland and to No. 3 in the UK when it was released in April. It was a significant moment in the group's brief history. It earnt them some much needed respect from their critics and laid valuable cement on the foundations of their fledgling careers. More importantly, the success of their third single catapulted Boyzone into a new league of importance within their record company. They were now assured massive investment which included huge promotion for the début album, their first live tour of Ireland, and the UK and a major campaign in Europe and the Far East. The success of 'Key To My Life' also brought the lads their first financial rewards. The first two hits had helped pay back the initial investment to get Boyzone rolling and, until then, the lads were as broke as they had been before they were famous. It had been an odd situation: they were stars, with hit records behind them, yet there had been no noticeable change in their bank balances. They had been living off pocketmoney given to them by Louis, but that didn't go far. When they signed the deal for the album, however, all the lads were paid a substantial advance, which allowed them to buy cars and put some money in the bank. They were a long way from being rich, but they were certainly earning more than they would have done as mechanics or shop assistants, and the advance was just the start of a run of success that would make them all millionaires.

Boyzone worked continuously throughout the summer of 1995. They recorded the *Said And Done* album, which featured seven of their own songs and six cover versions. They toured Ireland and the UK, appearing at music festivals, radio roadshows, and signing sessions in every main city. They also made their first major promotional trips to Germany and other countries in central Europe where their singles had been a success. Wherever they went in the UK, they were greeted by loyal fans and their live radio gigs earnt them further respect within the pop media. Slowly, the cynics began to accept that Boyzone had talent, as well as mass appeal. The only bad news during this period came when Shane broke his left ankle after jumping over a narrow stream to fetch a basketball. It was a moment of bad luck which threatened to disrupt plans for their autumn concert tour, but Shane vowed to continue despite the injury.

Although Boyzone were enjoying huge success, they were still firmly in the shadow of the seemingly unstoppable Take That. The Manchester band scored yet another instant No. 1 in July 1995 with the release of 'Never Forget'. But the mood of the song gave a clue that the mighty juggernaut may just be coming to the end of its incredible journey. In the lyrics, Gary Barlow reflected on the years of triumph and admitted that it was all destined to end some day when it would become someone else's dream. They were poignant words from the driving force behind Take That and indicated that maybe the group was running out of steam. The problems within Take That were graphically displayed when, soon after the release of 'Never Forget', Robbie Williams suddenly left. It emerged there had been bitter rows behind the scenes and that not everything had been as happy as the band's public façade had presented. The news of Robbie's departure shocked Boyzone. They weren't happy to see him leave in such sad and negative circumstances, but it was undeniable, however, that the fragmentation of Take That could only work to Boyzone's advantage.

The five Irish lads proved they were already a force to be reckoned with alongside Take That when their new single, 'So Good', went to No. 3 and the *Said And Done* album went straight to No. 1. The record company laid on a special press launch at one of Britain's biggest theme parks, Chessington World of Adventures, where all the VIP guests were given a free run of the park. It was an appropriate venue. Most children dream of being given the freedom of a fun fair and, in a way, it was happening to Boyzone on a far wider and more exciting scale as they enjoyed the most exhilarating rollercoaster ride of their lives. The thrills continued after the album launch with their first live concert tour of the UK. Despite Shane hobbling on with his left foot in plaster, every gig was a sell-out and a huge success, culminating with a sensational last night at London's Royal Albert Hall.

Even after an exhausting tour, there was no time to rest as the boys were whisked off on a whistle-stop tour of Europe and then the Far East, including visits to Thailand, Hong Kong, Korea and Japan. Some of the lads had never even been abroad before they joined the band, yet now they were clocking thousands of miles across the globe.

One of Boyzone's proudest triumphs came at the end of that year with the success of their single 'Father And Son', a poignant song for the band, especially Ronan. It had been the song which Ronan had loved as a little boy; it had inspired his interest in music and, ultimately, his pursuit of pop fame; later, the song had secured his place in Boyzone when he sang it for Louis Walsh at the auditions. It was also one of the first songs the band did together and they had accepted it as their anthem. To all of them, it was *the* Boyzone song. Now the emotional tune had captured the hearts of their fans as it went to No. 2 in the charts in the UK and into the top-ten in more than ten other countries.

'Father And Son' stayed in the UK charts for fourteen weeks and brought praise from its writer Cat Stevens. It also prompted the owners of London's Rock Circus to acknowledge Boyzone by inviting them to have their hands cast in the Wall of Hands, an honour previously bestowed upon music greats such as Michael Jackson and Eric Clapton.

At the *Smash Hits* Poll Winners' Party, Boyzone won tributes and collected the Best Album Award while Steve was voted Best Dressed Man of 1995. They were two well-deserved awards, but the lads had to sit back and watch Take That pick up the customary collection of trophies. Take That were still the kings of pop, but the pretenders to the throne weren't envious. Boyzone had enjoyed a fantastic year and deep down they knew that 1996 would be their coronation year.

10

BOYZONEMANIA

If Boyzone thought 1995 had been busy, they were in for a shock with the work load in 1996. Louis Walsh had prepared a gruelling schedule for the band's wider global expansion, which would see them cover many more thousands of miles; the lads who had hardly travelled before Boyzone were fast becoming experts at coping with jet-lag and passing through international time zones, although they all maintained a strict intake of vitamin pills to keep them healthy.

Boyzone were destined to stay firmly in the jet stream for the year. The main target was to make their first in-roads in America and really dominate Europe and the Far East. But, as well as building on their popularity abroad, they began planning their first arena tour of the UK, and writing material for their second album. Their tour agent, Louis Parker, had initially started booking 2,000-seater venues, but the success of Boyzone had created a stampede for tickets. Louis says, 'When tickets went on sale, the whole lot sold out in a single day – that's when we realised we could put them in arenas.'

The year started positively when they received an unexpected nomination in the Best International Newcomer category at the Brit Awards, one of the most prestigious ceremonies within the music business. They didn't win, but the mere inclusion alongside the cream of the world's rock and pop acts was a welcome boost for a band which had once been so widely derided within the business. There was more good news when Boyzone's new single, 'Coming Home', went to No. 3 in the UK. It was another original tune which was inspired by their feelings when they returned to Ireland after spending so many months on the road. Steve says 'We love travelling but, no matter where we go, we all really miss Ireland. This song is about how much we love our home and our families.'

'Coming Home' was released at the same time as Take That's new song, a cover version of the Bee Gees' 1977 hit 'How Deep Is Your Love'. Typically, Take That took top honours and went straight to No. 1, but their sweet victory was soured soon after when Gary Barlow, Mark Owen, Jason Orange and Howard Donald called an urgent press conference to confirm rumours that would break the hearts of their fans worldwide: they were splitting up.

The first chinks in Take That's armour had appeared when Robbie left the previous year. Now it emerged they all felt the band had gone as far as it could and they wanted to quit at the top, rather than continue on to a less dignified exit. Gary Barlow, in particular, was bored and wanted to focus on his solo career. The end of the Fab Five was sad for their fans, but it was great news for Boyzone. Ronan and the lads weren't happy to see such a talented group break up; after all, if it hadn't been for the inspiration of Take That's success, Boyzone may never have even existed. But now their arch rivals were off the scene, the way ahead was clear for Boyzone to climb to the very top of the pop mountain.

Just how near Boyzone already were to the summit was confirmed within days of Take That's announcement. They appeared in Dublin for a signing session at the HMV record store for the new single, and the city's main shopping thoroughfare was brought to a standstill by more than 6,000 hysterical fans. Extra police were needed to organise the crowds to avoid a dangerous stampede and it took five hours for Boyzone to complete the signing session. The group needed no further confirmation of their popularity among fans, but it was comforting to find out soon after the HMV hysteria that the music industry was also ready to acknowledge their success. Boyzone were honoured at the Irish Music Awards with trophies for the Best Irish Band and Best Irish Single for 'Key To My Life' in a glittering ceremony in Dublin. As the Take That tidal wave ebbed away, it was clear the next swell to fill its place was already gaining mighty strength.

Although Boyzone enjoyed their fame, it was bringing enormous pressure on their families. They were beginning to get angry with the constant attention from devoted fans who would stake out their homes, even when the boys were away working. It became a constant source of annoyance to the boys' parents and brothers and sisters as they tried to continue their normal lives, only to find up to a dozen or more girls in the street hoping for a glimpse of their idol. Boyzone themselves had become familiar with being shadowed by fans and had learnt to cope with the pressure, but they felt it wasn't fair for their families to lose their privacy as well. Keith snapped, 'We like the attention but it's not on for our families to be bothered all the time. I hope the fans will respect their privacy.'

Fame may have made Boyzone heart-throbs with countless girls craving their attention, but, sadly, in reality it ruined any chance of serious romance for Ronan, Steve and Shane. It was an odd contradiction: they were the subject of adoration and girls' dreams, yet they were single and finding it almost impossible to fall in love. Now they were pop stars, how could they know if a girl wanted them for their real character, or simply for their fame and wealth? The situation was particularly difficult for Ronan, who admitted in an interview that he is still a virgin and has never had a serious girlfriend. He was brought up in a strict Catholic faith which prohibits sex before marriage. He's happy to stick to those religious rules, but is acutely aware how stardom, and his whirlwind lifestyle, have further complicated his chances of finding love. In one interview he said, 'It's hard being away from my family and I can feel so lonely. I don't have a girlfriend and I sometimes wish I had someone to rely on, someone to talk to. I often lie awake at night and wonder when I'm going to meet the girls of my dreams. I'm a romantic and I'm still waiting for the perfect girl. Believe me, being in a pop band doesn't make it any easier. Relationships are out of the question right now because we are too busy and it just wouldn't be fair on any girl to put up with our hectic lifestyle.

'I tell the fans I'm a virgin and they know to look, but not to touch. A one-night stand isn't how I plan to lose my virginity. It's a very special thing to me. I come from a good Catholic family and was brought up to respect it. When the girls get fruity, I stand my ground and tell them I have to wait for the special moment when I know it will be right. When it is, I know that girl will be my only sexual partner. Call me idealistic, but I know it's achievable. If you love somebody, anything is possible. Love is the most abused word in the world and is too often used and said for the wrong reasons.

'I used to laugh at the kids at school who slept around. They showed no respect by wasting something so important. When I hear about lads coming home from a two-week holiday in Majorca, where they put it about, I think it's pathetic. I just wasn't brought up to think like that. Some of my classmates were parents before they finished school – that would have scared the life out of me. I'm almost permanently shocked by the upfront activities of some of the fans and I spend half my life being embarrassed at what's happening to me. I'm a virgin and that's the way I want to stay for the time being. The thought of going to bed with someone you hardly know terrifies me.'

Steve and Shane aren't virgins but they faced similar problems finding a girlfriend they can trust. The same, however, hasn't been true of Keith and Mikey and it emerged in the press that they were both already involved in serious relationships. Keith met a local Dublin girl called Lisa Smith at the POD disco in 1994 and they had remained together throughout his time in Boyzone. They were photographed together on holiday in Tenerife by a paparazzi photographer but the 'scandal' of a teen heart-throb having a girlfriend blew over.

Mikey, too, had met the love of his life – Sharon Keane – in a nightclub before he joined the group. Louis Walsh had banned both lads from talking publicly about their relationships in case it would upset the fans, but he could no longer suppress the truth when it was revealed Mikey and Keith were living with their partners and were about to become fathers! Starting a family while being in a top pop group is hardly the best career move, but Lisa and Sharon were both expecting babies in April, shortly before the start of Boyzone's long-awaited arena tour. The timing couldn't have been much worse and it threw the future of the band into doubt. How could two members continue to be dedicated pop stars while they were young dads?

The babies arrived within a few days of each other and both Mikey and Keith dashed from rehearsals for the tour to be with their girlfriends. Lisa gave birth to a baby boy, who they called Jordan, after Keith's favourite American basketball player, Michael Jordan. Sharon had a baby girl, who they named Hannah. Many Boyzone fans were shocked to learn of the Babyzone within the band, especially after being led to believe for so long that all the singers were single. But their anger subsided when Mikey and Keith pledged their loyalty to Boyzone above their babies. As far as they were concerned, fatherhood would have to take a back seat while they devoted themselves to the continuing success of the group. Their immediate priority wasn't nappy changing, but making sure the new tour was a hit.

The tour kicked off in a small venue on the Northern coast of Wales. It was a low-key start to what would escalate into Boyzone's biggest and most triumphant tour to date. The lads unveiled a simple, but effective stage set of wire mesh and steel stairways leading to a twelve-metre-high gantry, all of which evoked a gritty street scene. In contrast to the simplicity of the backdrop, they thrilled the 1,030 audience at the Pavilion Theatre in Rhyl with an hour and a half of breathless, complicated dance routines and costume changes. It was their first tour with their own live band and it worked brilliantly. They began in silver jackets and cool dark glasses for their opening number, 'Together', and belted through a series of fast numbers. They then slipped into smart pin-stripe suits for a mellow section, including 'Arms Of Mary', 'Father And Son' and 'Key To My Life'. They followed this with further costume changes before ending the gig with a moving rendition of 'Love Me For A Reason' and the final song, 'Coming Home'. It was a stunning show, which featured all the band's hits and tracks from *Said And Done* and left the fans exhilarated and longing to see Boyzone again.

The opening at Rhyl was just a warm-up and was organised mainly because the band's tour agent, Louis Parker, grew up in the coastal tourist destination and booked Britain's hottest act there as a favour to his hometown. After that date, the exhausting tour schedule began in earnest. The boys covered thousands of miles criss-crossing Britain and Ireland, playing fifty concerts at thirty-five venues. On average they performed in front of 5,000 fans at each arena and each night they received standing ovations and chants for more. Everywhere Boyzone travelled, they were greeted by hysterical fans snapping photographs, scrambling for autographs and waving banners. Some of the cheekier messages were: 'Shane, Show Us Your Lynchbox', 'Keith, Keith, Get Me Beneath', 'Ronan, You Are So-oo-Good' and 'Irish Boyz Do It Best'.

The music critics, too, had flattering words to write. They welcomed the tour with praise and a British tabloid review of one London gig summed up the band's incredible progression. It said: 'As Take That fade away, will Boyzone steal their crown? From the reception of their current tour, it's clear they are well on the way to reigning supreme. The moment the five boys, in snazzy silver suits, burst on to the stage, the audience went wild with delight. The lads' bare chests and sexy dance routines worked the screaming fans into a frenzy. Ronan Keating, with his superb voice, emerged as the star of the show. Catch Boyzone on this tour and get set for the latest teen sensation.'

The boys took great pride in their stage show and were determined to give their fans value for money. Ronan says, 'We don't just go on stage and sing. Our show is like a seduction scene, it's a bit like picking up a girl at a party – you don't just crash in, you chat them up, flirt a little, dance like crazy, have a couple of smooches, then finish up with a real boogie. We have a fantastic stage set which is like a backstreet scene. We go through four costume changes, do a lot of dance routines and give absolutely everything. We could cut corners but that would be cheating our fans.'

As Boyzone lapped up the glory on their arena tour, the fate of the two original Boyzone members who were left behind was revealed. Richie Rock, who had been sacked a week before the band secured their record deal, was finding it hard to cope with the legacy of having been part of Boyzone, only to miss out on the big time. He was unemployed and trying to get back into the music business. Still living with his parents in Dublin, he had mixed feelings about his time with the group and bitterly regretted ruining his chance of fame. Richie says, 'Seeing Boyzone become so massive makes everything so hard for me to deal with. I saw them on breakfast television the other morning introducing their new song and I thought, 'Why am I sitting here in my living room watching this? I should be on the TV looking out at everyone else.

'It's been tough and I often cry because I'm so angry at what has happened. I think about what could have been every single day of my life. It's even worse at the moment because my car is broke and I have to walk which gives me even more time to think. Kids around Dublin still recognise me and ask, "Why aren't you with Boyzone anymore?" It tears me to pieces. I often stare at photos of me in Boyzone for hours on end before I snap out of it. But they have worked really hard for everything, so they deserve it. I lost belief in the band in the early days. I just wish I had hung in there a little bit longer. Being a pop star is everything I wanted in life, but I blew it.'

In contrast, Mark Walton is more positive about his time in Boyzone. He was the lad who dreamed up the whole idea, but left because he couldn't cope with the pressure of fame. He went back to school and passed all his exams with honours and, only then did he decide to have another go at finding fame in a boy band. He was head-hunted by a manager who was impressed with his dancing skills, and a new group was built around him. The end result was Only Us, a mixed race four-piece band, which scored two chart hits and was voted the Best New Boy Band in Ireland in 1996. Mark is philosophical about Boyzone and hopeful that Only Us will succeed. He says, 'At times it has been hard to see the lads make it so big. I have watched them on MTV and thought, "My God, that could be me up there being a star, not sitting at home." But when I was in Boyzone, I couldn't cope with the strain and ended up in tears at night. I was too young and too scared. I can honestly say I'm not bitter. I love those guys and I'm happy and proud of everything they have achieved. I'm still great friends with Ronan and Shane and will be celebrating with them when they come home for Christmas. I'm still remembered by fans in Dublin for my part in Boyzone so the band follows me around like a ghost. Thankfully, it's a friendly ghost.

'After leaving Boyzone I went back to school, but it was difficult going back to a normal life. Three weeks after I left Boyzone, they released the single and were stars overnight. 'I would cringe watching them on MTV, or *Top Of The Pops*, after I'd had a bad day at school. I would think, Jesus, why am I sitting here studying when I could be on the telly having a good time with the lads. It was depressing and really confusing.

'It was odd because I still had loads of fans even though I wasn't in the band. I got a job in the Levi's store in Dublin but I had to quit because some days I would have twenty girls in the shop taking pictures and asking for my autograph. The manager said, "This is crazy, you'll have to go." It was a mad situation. I was still getting the attention of a pop star, but I wasn't enjoying the glamour of that life. Despite everything, I can honestly say I have never cried about being out of Boyzone, or that the guys are making so much money. I still feel deep down that it all happened for a reason.

'Being good friends with Ronan and Shane makes it easier – they are like brothers to me. All the lads are genuinely nice guys who don't forget who their old friends are. They know the score and fair play to them for everything they have achieved. I'm happy I played a part in it all and I'm glad they have done our country proud. I decided I wanted to have another go in the music business. I got some good singing lessons and went to the gym three times a week. I got myself physically and mentally fit, so I would be ready this time round.

'At first I did a lot of dancing at various events and built up a bigger fan base. I had several managers chasing me. They thought I had talent and then we started Only Us. Things have really taken off for us recently. Our First single went to No. 8 and we were just voted the best new boy band. It's full speed ahead now. Ronan and Shane have been very supportive. They like what we are doing and have given me advice on all kinds of things. They'd be honest with me if they didn't like our music.

'I wasn't ready for this life when I was with Boyzone, but now I love having thousands of girls screaming at me. I'm far more relaxed and happy with it all. It would be the best thing in the world if we made it in the UK. I reckon all the lads in Boyzone would be pleased for us, too. So watch your back, guys!'

The climax to Boyzone's summer tour was at Wembley Arena, in North London, where they played in front of thousands on three consecutive nights. The reception at each concert was incredible and underlined how far Boyzone had come in just over two years. During the final gigs, the fans were treated to a sneak preview of the group's latest material from the forthcoming second album, *A Different Beat*, and the reaction proved Boyzone were on the right track for another massive hit album.

The final costs for the tour came in at just under £2 million and its organisers estimated that each singer would earn little more than £20,000 for their work. That may not seem a huge pay cheque for a hot national pop tour, but it was in addition to their basic £700-a-week wages, and their total earnings were expected to more than double once the revenue from merchandising had been shared out. But Boyzone weren't completely focused on the balance sheet. Sure, the money was nice, but they had already made a considerable amount out of Boyzone. Most of them had bought their own homes, endless racks of designer clothes and flash sports cars. Even car-mad Shane was becoming bored of his Porsche. He says, 'The other day I was actually thinking of selling my Porsche because I've been there, done that. It was a novelty, but now it's like, "Yeah, I'm driving a Porsche – give me a bloody Toyota and I can get there just as quick!"'

No, the tour wasn't about hard cash – it was an investment to secure them a greater following and, on that score, they were deeply in the black. The one person, however, who did feel slightly out of pocket when the tour finished was Keith: his bar bill alone was £6,000! He says: 'I buy drinks for everyone in the bar after the shows and lose track of what I'm spending. On the next tour, I'm not going to drink – I'll save a fortune.'

Further riches were secured for Boyzone on 13 October 1996 when they chalked up their first UK No. 1 with their single 'Words', a cover version of the Bee Gees 1967 hit. This success was swiftly followed by the release of the second album, *A Different Beat*, which also went straight to the top. Boyzone were hotter than ever and it boosted the hype in the media which even saw the 'serious' newspapers devoting pages to the Boyzone phenomenon. But it emerged in the press that all hadn't been so sweet and happy behind the scenes for the band, especially during the making of the album and leading up to its release. Tensions had risen between the lads and their record company. The band had initially wanted to release the title track of the album as the first single, but were over-ruled and 'Words' was brought out instead. In the early days of Boyzone, Ronan and the others did everything they were told, but now they felt like veterans of the pop world. They had matured and were confident of the direction the band should take and were determined to make their own decisions. In an interview with *Smash Hits*, Boyzone spoke candidly about the secrets behind the months leading up to the album.

Ronan said, 'People blame us for releasing a cover. They don't realise the record company or the managers have their say, too. Obviously people will say, "Another cover version?" But what's wrong with a cover? People can sing along better. The single after this, "A Different Beat", will tell all – it'll show we can write our own stuff. We went through a very testing time this summer but we have come out on top. It was good for us, very healthy. We're much better mates for it now. We're really happy and looking foward to this album. We're gonna show people where we've been and where we're going.'

The lads didn't elaborate on the tensions and all Keith would say was: 'Everyone was doing little annoying things to wind each other up, not even intentionally.' Whatever the problems, they seemed well and truly forgotten when Boyzone appeared at the *Smash Hits* Poll Winner's Party and swept the board. They collected six awards: Best International Group, Best Album for *A Different Beat*, Best Single for 'Words', and Ronan picked up a hat trick of trophies for Best Haircut, Best Dressed Person and Most Fanciable Male. It was a remarkable collection, which beat The Spice Girls into second place with three awards. The excitement proved a little too much for the man of the moment, Ronan. Shortly after performing 'Words' for the 14,000-strong audience, he collapsed. Manager Louis Walsh said at the time: 'Ronan has had a very hectic schedule and had nothing to eat all day. We think he's OK now, but I'll probably give him a day or two off.'

Ronan did recover quickly to enjoy the rest of the *Smash Hits* party, but, a few days later, as Boyzone prepared for extra concert dates in key cities, he reflected on the strain of being Britain's greatest heart-throb. He says: 'I went a bit dizzy after the *Smash Hits* awards ceremony in London and my mum was straight on the phone after reading about it in the newspapers. She always looks after me. She rang up and said, "I'm getting on the next flight over. I'm going to cook you a proper dinner."

'I have acute bronchitis and I'm on antibiotics. I do feel a bit ill and the doctors want me to take it easy. I should be resting but I can't because we have more shows to do and I'm certainly not going to let the fans down. I lost my voice during the week and that really scared me. I thought, "Oh, my God, this can't be happening to me". But it came back. Sure I feel pretty rough right now that but that's not going to stop me.'

Ronan got the ideal tonic for his poor health a few days later when the single 'A Different Beat' went straight to No. 1 on 8 December. It was a sweet moment, given the difficult background to the song's release. But, the celebrations were short-lived: the following week Boyzone were kicked off the top by 'Knockin' On Heaven's Door', the single released by the children of Dunblane in memory of the tragic shooting of sixteen children and their teacher at the primary school. Boyzone were happy to give up their No. 1 spot for the Dunblane cause and as 'A Different Beat' slipped to No. 4 they sent a fax: 'Congratulations on a No. 1 record. Our thoughts and best wishes go to you and your families this Christmas. God bless, Boyzone.'

As 1996 drew to a close, Boyzone toasted a truly magnificent year. It had started with high expectations and confident predictions, particularly from their ever-confident manager Louis Walsh. Again, as Louis looked into his crystal ball for 1997, he predicted even greater worldwide success for Boyzone, with grander tours and more record sales. And who could doubt him? Louis had always talked a big game. Right from the start, when he was sifting through his batch of unknowns in 1993, he knew his answer to Take That could reign supreme. And his boys had never let him down. Louis had taken them from the obscurity of everyday lives in the Northside, to worldwide fame and fortune.

When they launched their début single 'Working My Way Back To You' in 1994 they were unknown, raw novices praying for a hit single. Now, they are without question the biggest teen pop group of the moment. They have notched up a collection of No. 1 and top-ten hits, two No. 1 albums, numerous awards and even praise from the cynics in the media. The lives of all the boys have changed beyond recognition, but they still enjoy their success. In one interview, they each explained what making it with Boyzone has meant to them and how it has changed them.

Mikey said, 'Joining Boyzone was the best move I could ever have made. At the time, I was in two minds because it meant leaving my family and leading a crazy life travelling around the world. But every minute has been worth it. I have had to grow up very quickly, because I now have a responsibility to so many other people, but I have had a ball.'

Keith said, 'I joined the group when I was nineteen and since then my life has changed dramatically. At the start, most people thought we were no good, but we have proved ourselves with our hits and our sell-out tours. One of the most important things to me is that Lisa gave me a little boy, but I still love each and every one of my fans – they are fantastic. The job can be hard at times, but we've been around the world and met a lot of interesting people. I know that if things had to suddenly change and I wasn't doing it any more, I'd miss it like mad.'

Steve said, 'I was just eighteen when I joined Boyzone and I had absolutely no idea what lay in store. I'd done jobs before, working in a shop and as a child actor, but this was obviously a chance for the big time. When I got the audition I had to work at getting to know the others, but after a while we all gelled together, and now we work as a slick machine. Despite what fans may think, I am still really shy underneath it all and I blush to think anyone could fancy me. I cope with the pace of life by having quiet times and I always room alone when we are on tour to keep me sane.'

Shane said, 'When I was young I always thought I would have a career in sports or as a car mechanic. All that went out the window when I joined the group. Since June 1994, I haven't had a single day off, but it has been a thrilling time. I have always been fairly quiet and I'm used to being in the background, so I've had to push myself forward to fit in. I'm still quiet and I think of myself as the strong, silent type and have never been one to brag about our success. Even though we hang around with other pop stars, stay in swanky hotels and lead very exciting lives, I have to confess that I still love the thought of going home to my parents, shutting the door behind me and having a normal chat over a cup of tea. I'm still a homeboy at heart and don't think that will ever change, no matter how successful I become.'

Finally, Ronan summed up. 'Being in Boyzone has changed me a great deal. I've had to grow up very fast and become an adult. I realise we're doing mad jobs and living in an unreal world. I've just been voted Top Male Idol, but when I look in the mirror, I don't see a heart-throb – just plain old Ro from Dublin. My hair has changed and I wear nice clothes, plus I've got a bit of money saved in the bank, but I like to think I'm still a good person and not big-headed. Besides, if I ever get a swollen ego, my mum will give me a hard clip around the ear.'

Rumours started flying around at the end of 1996 that Boyzone were on the verge of splitting, but these were vehemently denied and, as yet, have proved unfounded. The rise of Boyzone continues and has been truly phenomenal by anyone's standards. The five lads who grew up separately with varying dreams, were brought together by a blend of fate and skilful marketing. Thanks to good fortune, genuine talent, and sheer hard work, they have made those dreams come true and entertained thousands of their fans.

There are still people out there who scoff at Boyzone and their music, but no one can take away their achievements or deny that they are down-to-earth young men who took a major gamble forming their group and deserve every scream and every record sale. Good luck to Ronan, Mikey, Steve, Keith and Shane, and, hopefully, there is plenty more to come. . .

ABOUT THE AUTHOR

Rob McGibbon began his journalistic career on the *Wimbledon News*, in South London, and worked as a news reporter and showbusiness writer on several national newspapers before leaving to write books.

In 1990, he co-wrote the first biography of New Kids On The Block with his father, Robin, also a journalist. They gambled on publishing the book themselves, before the band were famous in Britain; it became a worldwide bestseller. In the next three years, they wrote biographies of England footballer Paul Gascoigne, TV presenter Phillip Schofield and Simply Red's lead singer Mick Hucknall. In addition, Rob wrote a biography of Take That, which was a bestseller in Germany, and *Boyzone on the Road* for Boxtree.

In between writing books, Rob is a freelance journalist mainly writing celebrity interviews for newspapers and international magazines. He lives in Chelsea, London. Among his many interests, apart from writing, is soccer and, as a life-long Chelsea fan, one of his proudest sporting moments was playing in a celebrity charity match at Stamford Bridge.

—